The Texas Revolution 1835–36

Texian Volunteer

VERSUS

Mexican Soldier

COMBAT

Ron Field

Illustrated by Steve Noon

OSPREY PUBLISHING
Bloomsbury Publishing Plc
Kemp House, Chawley Park, Cumnor Hill, Oxford OX2 9PH, UK
29 Earlsfort Terrace, Dublin 2, Ireland
1385 Broadway, 5th Floor, New York, NY 10018, USA
E-mail: info@ospreypublishing.com
www.ospreypublishing.com

OSPREY is a trademark of Osprey Publishing Ltd

First published in Great Britain in 2023

A catalog record for this book is available from the British Library.

ISBN: PB 9781472852076; eBook 9781472852007;
ePDF 9781472852014; XML 9781472851994

23 24 25 26 27   10 9 8 7 6 5 4 3 2 1

Maps by www.bounford.com
Index by Rob Munro
Typeset by PDQ Digital Media Solutions, Bungay, UK
Printed and bound in India by Replika Press Private Ltd.

Osprey Publishing supports the Woodland Trust, the UK's leading
woodland conservation charity.

To find out more about our authors and books visit
www.ospreypublishing.com. Here you will find extracts, author
interviews, details of forthcoming events and the option to sign up for
our newsletter.

Artist's note

Readers may care to note that the original paintings from which the
color plates in this book were prepared are available for private sale. All
reproduction copyright whatsoever is retained by the publishers. All
inquiries should be addressed to:

www.steve-noon.co.uk

The publishers regret that they can enter into no correspondence upon
this matter.

Acknowledgments

Kia L. Dorman, Registrar, Alamo Trust, Inc., San Antonio, TX; Lisa
A. Struthers, Library Director, Albert and Ethel Herzstein Library,
San Jacinto Museum and Battlefield Association, La Porte, TX; Carlos
Cortéz, Library Assistant III, UTSA Special Collections, University of
Texas at San Antonio, TX; Michelle Lambing, Graphics Coordinator,
State Preservation Board, Austin, TX; Kaitlyn Price, Registrar, Dallas
Historical Society, TX; The Archives Staff, Texas State Library and
Archives Commission, Austin, TX; Ali James, Curator of the Capitol
at the State Preservation Board, Austin, TX; Aryn Glazier, The Dolph
Briscoe Center for American History, Austin, TX; Matthew Rowe,
Library Services Assistant, Beinecke Rare Book and Manuscript Library,
Yale University, New Haven, CT; Peter Harrington, Curator, Anne
S.K. Brown Military Collection, Providence, Rhode Island; and René
Chartrand.

CONTENTS

Introduction

The battle cry "Remember the Alamo! Remember Goliad!" resounded along the line as Major General Sam Houston gave the order to advance on April 21, 1836. The effect was instantaneous as the Texian infantrymen stepped forward at the double-quick, with fifer Frederick Lemsky of Co. A, 1st Regt. Regular Infantry, playing "Will you come to the Bower" as they advanced toward the breastworks and campsite of the Mexican army commanded by General of Division Antonio López de Santa Anna. Caught by surprise, the Mexican troops panicked and ran as the Texians rushed toward them without firing a shot. Each Texian reserved his fire until he could choose his target at virtually point-blank range. Crashing into the Mexican encampment, the Texians then used their muskets and long rifles as clubs. Desperate hand-to-hand fighting developed in some quarters as Mexican officers attempted to rally their troops, while elsewhere Mexicans fled into the woods to the rear or ran into the marshland and waters of the San Jacinto River and McCormick's Lake. There they were shot down by their vengeful pursuers. With the defeat Santa Anna, the self-styled "Napoleon of the West" at San Jacinto and his capture the next day, the future of the Republic of Texas was assured.

Published in 1900 in *The Evolution of a State or Recollections of Old Texas Days* by Noah Smithwick, this sketch entitled "The Flying Artillery" was produced by Nanna Smithwick Donaldson, daughter of Noah Smithwick who took part in the action at Gonzales on October 6, 1835. It shows the makeshift gun carriage and limber made by the Texian volunteers and used in the skirmish at Gonzales, which provoked the campaign leading to the Alamo and beyond. The drover carries his musket suspended from leather straps over his shoulders. (Author's collection)

This reconstruction of the flag carried by Texians who fought at Gonzales in 1835 was produced by Nanna Smithwick Donaldson. It was described by Texian volunteer Noah Smithwick as "a breadth of white cotton cloth about 6ft long, in the center of which was painted in black a picture of the old cannon, above it a lone star and beneath it the words, 'Come and take it,' a challenge which was lost on the Mexicans" (Smithwick 1900: 105) (Author's collection)

The revolt that led to the Texas Revolution began in 1835 in the eastern part of the Mexican state of Coahuila and Texas among the Anglos and *Tejanos* (Hispanic settlers), collectively known as Texians (*NOB*, October 13, 1835: 2:1), and was caused by the dictatorial policies of President Anastasio Bustamante. Having been invited to colonize the sparsely populated land under Mexican jurisdiction according to the Constitution of 1824, which had created a federal representative republic, the Anglos became alarmed when the Laws of 1830 were introduced on April 6 that year. These prohibited further immigration to Texas from the United States of America, increased taxes, and reiterated the ban on slavery, which had been abolished by Mexico in 1829. Ignoring the Laws of 1830, slave-owning Anglo settlers continued to arrive in Texas. By 1834 an estimated 30,000 Anglos had settled there compared to only 7,800 *Tejanos*. Among the Anglos were almost 5,000

Produced in 1901 and entitled "Ben Milam Calling for Volunteers," this painting by Henry A. McArdle shows the Texian leader waving his slouch hat and rallying volunteers for an attack on San Antonio de Béxar on December 5, 1835. Reportedly flown in the Texian camp, the "Come and Take It" battle flag can be seen at far right. (Alamo Collection, San Antonio)

enslaved African Americans, whose existence there was in contravention of Mexican legislation.

As unrest grew in 1835, Santa Anna, who had been appointed president of Mexico on May 16, 1833, ordered all weapons issued to settlers in 1831 for protection against the depredations of the Comanche to be returned to government arsenals in case they were used by Anglos against his army. In September 1835, Anglos and some *Tejanos* gathered at Gonzales, in south central Texas, to stop Mexican troops from repossessing a bronze swivel gun supplied to them.

When the initial request to return the gun was refused, Colonel Domingo de Ugartechea, commander of all Mexican troops in Texas, sent 150 Presidial cavalrymen under Captain Francisco de Castañeda, from his headquarters at San Antonio de Béxar to seize it. As the cavalry neared Gonzales, the settlers sent messengers asking for assistance from nearby Texian communities. Within several days, approximately 140 Texians, including lawyer and soldier William B. Travis and slave-trader James W. Fannin, Jr., had gathered in Gonzales, determined not to give up the gun, which they had concealed by burying it. On October 1, 1835, they voted to initiate hostilities against the Mexican troops in defense of the Constitution of 1824. Electing as their colonel John W. Moore, and armed with "Bowie knives and long single-barreled, muzzle-loading flintlock rifles" (Smithwick 1900: 104), they dug up the gun and mounted it, and a crudely made limber, on wooden carriages with wheels cut from two slices of tree trunk. This was placed under the command of Captain of Artillery James C. Neill and Almeron Dickinson, a blacksmith and former artilleryman in the US Army.

The Texians advanced on the Mexicans during the early hours of October 6. Years later, Creed Taylor, one of the volunteers who marched that day, recalled that the little army was not organized for fighting and lacked a commissary, quartermaster, medical corps, and baggage train, but it did carry a makeshift flag. Crossing the Guadalupe River, it attempted to surprise the Mexican cavalry in their camp, but thick fog prevented the Texians from discovering the Mexicans' exact position until the alarm was raised and, after exchanging shots, the Mexican commander withdrew his men to high ground. According Dr. Joseph E. Field, one of the Texians volunteers, when the fog lifted Moore sent Castañeda a challenge to come and "try the right of property by powder and ball. But they declining and being mounted, while we were on foot, we could only send them a parting benediction from the mouth of the cannon which they came to take" (*CC*, August 20, 1836: 1:1). In this action, two Mexican soldiers were killed, and one Texian was injured when he fell off his horse.

With the Mexican cavalry returning to San Antonio de Béxar, about 75 miles to the west,

Stephen F. Austin commanded Texian forces at the successful siege of San Antonio de Béxar after which he served as a commissioner to the United States. He ran in the 1836 Texas presidential election but was defeated by Samuel Houston, who appointed him Secretary of State for the new republic. He held that position until his death from pneumonia on December 27, 1836. (National Portrait Gallery, Smithsonian Institution, NPG-9300782A_2)

the Texians returned to Gonzales to prepare for further combat. Although this skirmish had little military importance, it signified a clear break between the settlers and the Mexican government and is considered the start of the Texas Revolution. As news of the action spread throughout the United States, numerous newspapers referred to it as the "Lexington of Texas," likening the action at Gonzales to the battles of Lexington and Concord that began the American Revolution (*MFT*, November 3, 1835: 3:2).

As a result of the action on October 6, scores of adventurers flocked to Texas from the United States to join the fight. Continuing to assemble at Gonzales, they established the "Army of the People," and despite a lack of military training, well-respected local leader Stephen F. Austin was elected their commander five days later. Determined to drive the Mexican army out of Texas, the Texians prepared to march on San Antonio de Béxar.

Learning that Texians had attacked Castañeda's command at Gonzales, General of Brigade Martin Perfecto de Cos, brother-in-law of Santa Anna, marched from his headquarters at Presidio La Bahía in Goliad to San Antonio de Béxar escorted by a battalion of lancers, declaring he would "collect the revenue, disarm the citizens, establish a military government, and confiscate the property of the rebellious" (*CDLL*, October 13, 1835: 3:1).

Unaware of his departure, Texians in Matagorda at the mouth of the Colorado River, led by planter George M. Collinsworth, marched on Goliad in hopes of capturing Cos and seizing $50,000 in specie he had to pay the wages of his troops. On October 10, approximately 125 Texian volunteers stormed the presidio. During a 30-minute battle, three Mexican soldiers were killed and seven wounded; 24 were captured but the rest of the garrison under Captain Francisco Sandoval escaped. The Texian victory at Goliad cut off communication for Mexican forces between San Antonio de Béxar and the Gulf of Mexico and secured the Texians valuable arms and supplies, including two brass cannon, 500 muskets and carbines, 600 pikes, and several horses (*NOCB*, November 11, 1835: 2:2).

The Texians consolidated their position in Presidio La Bahía, and command was handed over to Captain Philip Dimmitt, who immediately ordered all the local volunteers to join Austin on the march to San Antonio de Béxar. At the end of October, Dimmitt sent 80 men under Captain Ira J. Westover southwest to capture Fort Lipantitlán, opposite San Patricio, on the Nueces River. Learning that most of the Mexican garrison were out looking for him, Westover pushed on by forced march and reached the fort late on November 3. Taken by surprise, the remaining 21-man Mexican garrison surrendered without firing a shot on condition of parole. Also captured were several small cannon. The bulk of the garrison, consisting

This hand-colored version of an engraving of General of Division Antonio López de Santa Anna was published in 1905 in *The History of our Country* by Edward S. Ellis and is based on a lithograph by Nicolas E. Maurin. According to the 1831 Mexican regulations, the gala or dress uniform for generals and field-grade officers consisted of a dark-blue wool coat with scarlet collar, wide lapels, turnbacks, cuffs, and piping. A 1in-wide row of gold embroidery consisting of intertwined laurels, palms, and olives decorated the collar and rear pocket flaps, and also edged the lapels and cuffs. Generals of division had two rows of embroidery on their cuffs and generals of brigade had one. The straps of gold epaulets had an embroidered metallic silver eagle and heavy bullion fringe secured to the shoulder by embroidered loops. (GRANGER – Historical Pictures Archive/Alamy Stock Photo)

This engraving of General of Brigade Martin Perfecto de Cos was published in 1887 in *Our Pioneers and their Daring Deeds* by D.M. Kelsey. (Author's collection)

of 73 men, returned next day and engaged the Texians in a half-hour firefight after which the Mexicans were driven off with a loss of 28 killed, wounded, or missing. One of Westover's men was wounded in the hand. With this victory, Texian forces controlled the Gulf Coast and threatened the port city of Matamoros, forcing Mexican commanders to send overland all communication with the Mexican interior. This slower route meant Cos was unable to request or receive reinforcements or supplies quickly.

Meanwhile, on October 16 Austin halted the march of his 450-strong army about 25 miles from San Antonio de Béxar, and sent a messenger to Cos requesting that he lay down his arms in order to avoid further bloodshed and civil war. Replying that he would not yield to the dictates of foreigners, Cos ordered his 650-strong garrison to build barricades throughout the town. Within days the Texian army initiated a rather loose siege of the city. On October 27, a mounted party of 92 Texians led by Colonel James Bowie and Fannin ran into a stronger Mexican cavalry patrol at Mission Concepción, about 2 miles from San Antonio de Béxar. Realizing he outnumbered the Texians, Ugartechea ordered an attack, which developed into a running fight as the Texians fell back. Showing considerable skill as a commander, Bowie sought cover in a gully where his men dismounted and held off three Mexican cavalry charges plus bombardment from a small cannon. After a 30-minute action and having sustained heavy casualties, Ugartechea's force withdrew to San Antonio de Béxar. Seizing the initiative, Bowie ordered a pursuit of the Mexicans during which he captured their gun. One Texian died at Mission Concepción, while 67 Mexican soldiers were killed and 35 wounded.

Elsewhere, on November 3, 1835, a meeting known as The Consultation was held by the Texians at San Felipe de Austin. Although some of the more radical delegates demanded an immediate declaration of independence, the moderates, including Austin and Houston, pointed out that such a course would alienate liberals in Mexico and the many *Tejanos* who had joined them in rebellion. After further debate, they cited their loyalty to the Constitution of 1824 and established a provisional government for a proposed state of Texas within the Mexican Republic. A prominent settler, Henry Smith, was elected as provisional governor, and a council was created to serve as a legislature. Measures were taken to establish a military force, with Houston as commander with the rank of major general. A navy was also established, and appeals were made for volunteers with generous land grants as reward for their service. Most importantly, diplomatic missions were sent to the United States, with Austin as one of three commissioners. With its work done, the Consultation adjourned on November 14; it would reconvene at

Washington-on-the-Brazos on March 1, 1836, and signed the Declaration of Independence the next day.

Continuing the siege of San Antonio de Béxar, the Texians began to suffer as the weather turned colder and rations dwindled. Small groups of them began to abandon the cause and returned home. Morale was boosted on November 18, however, when the first of two uniformed volunteer companies called the New Orleans Greys joined them from the United States. On November 26, scouts informed Colonel Edward Burleson, who had replaced Austin as commander, that a Mexican supply train, accompanied by 50–100 troops, was within 5 miles of San Antonio de Béxar. Sent to intercept them, Texian volunteers under Bowie and William H. Jack fought a short action that became known as the "Grass Fight," following which the Mexicans fled into San Antonio de Béxar, leaving behind their cargo of mainly horse fodder.

Although this small victory briefly lifted Texian spirits, morale continued to ebb away as the weather grew colder. Following several proposals to take San Antonio de Béxar by force being voted down, Burleson proposed on December 4 that the Texians retreat to Goliad and renew the siege next spring. In a last effort to avoid a retreat, Colonel Benjamin R. Milam recruited men to participate in an attack. During the early hours of the following morning, he advanced into the city at the head of about 200 Texians. Four days of

Situated on the southwest side of the San Antonio River, Presidio La Bahía in Goliad served as the Mexican headquarters in Texas at the beginning of the War of Independence in 1810, and was named "Fort Defiance" after its capture by Texians on October 10, 1835. One of the oldest churches in the Americas, the chapel within its compound, named "Our Lady of Loreto," was used as a magazine during the Texian occupation. (Library of Congress LC-DIG-highsm-29290)

MAP KEY

The battles featured in this book took place in the eastern part of the Mexican state of Coahuila and Texas, which became the Republic of Texas on March 2, 1836. Following the revolt against Mexican rule which began at Gonzales on October 6, 1835, Texians besieged San Antonio de Béxar, forcing General of Brigade Martin Perfecto de Cos to surrender and causing General of Division Antonio López de Santa Anna to march his Army of Operations north to quell the revolt. Texian forces under Colonel James Bowie and Lieutenant Colonel William B. Travis strengthened the defenses in the Alamo. They were besieged by Santa Anna's army on February 23, and were spared no quarter when the Alamo fell on March 6, 1836.

Following the Mexican victory at the Alamo, many Texians retreated toward the United States in what became known as the "Runaway Scrape," while Santa Anna ordered a three-pronged advance northeast through Texas. General of Brigade José de Urrea continued his march along the south coast with c.1,400 men; Brevet General of Brigade Antonio Gaona advanced across the northern reaches with a column of c.700 men; while Santa Anna and General of Brigade Joaquin Ramirez y Sesma marched through the center of Texas with c.1,200 men. As forces under Urrea advanced toward Goliad after minor successes at San Patricio (February 27) and Agua Dulce (March 2), Colonel James W. Fannin, Jr., delayed evacuating Fort Defiance until March 19, 1836, by which time Mexican forces were within sight. The Mexicans caught up with Fannin's retreating column near Coleto Creek the same day and a battle ensued until darkness fell. With the arrival of Mexican artillery, Fannin was forced to surrender the next day.

Believing the rebellion was in its final death throes, Santa Anna considered he had the Texian army under Major General Sam Houston cornered near Lynch's Ferry on the San Jacinto River and, after an initial skirmish on April 20, 1836, prepared for battle. Houston took Santa Anna's army completely by surprise by attacking and decisively defeating it the next day, capturing Santa Anna and much of his army.

intense fighting followed as the Texians fought their way from house to house, literally battering their way through walls, toward the fortified plaza and Church of San Fernando near the center of town.

On December 8, Cos received 650 reinforcements, most of whom were raw recruits and convicts still in chains, and all of whom proved a drain on his dwindling food supplies. The next day he withdrew with most of his command into the Alamo Mission on the outskirts north of the town. Despite proposing a counterattack, his cavalry officers refused to obey orders and, with about 175 troopers, broke out and rode south. Cos accepted surrender terms on December 11, by which he agreed to lead his command out of Texas and no longer fight against supporters of the Constitution of 1824. On his return to Mexico City, Cos was treated as a hero:

> We feel the greatest pleasure in making known that the brave and honorable General Cos is safe. Compelled by force of circumstances and scarcity of provisions, he capitulated, leaving the town of Bejar in possession of the rebels. He quitted that place with 560 men after having sustained a siege of 56 days. The conduct of General Cos, his officers and soldiers, need no comment, it does them as much honor as if they had obtained the greatest victory. (*ES*, February 1, 1836: 2:4)

With the departure of Cos, there was no longer an organized garrison of Mexican troops in Texas and all were forced to retreat beyond the Rio Grande River. As a result, many Texians believed the war was over. Burleson resigned his command of the army on December 15 and returned to his home. Many other men did likewise, and Frank W. Johnson assumed command of the 400 soldiers who remained in what became the Republic of Texas on March 2, 1836.

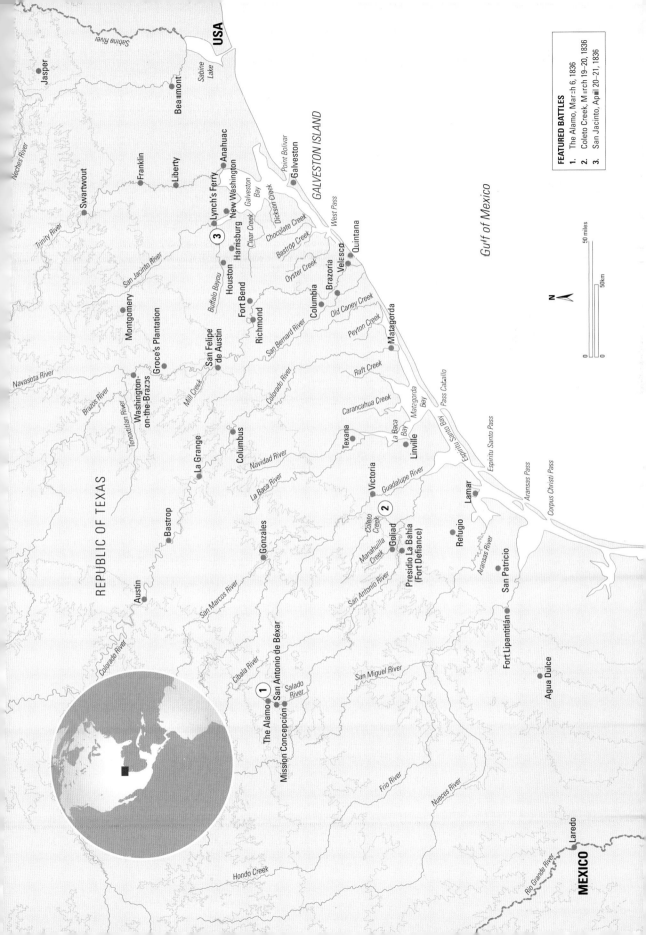

FEATURED BATTLES

1. The Alamo, March 6, 1836
2. Coleto Creek, March 19–20, 1836
3. San Jacinto, April 20–21, 1836

REPUBLIC OF TEXAS

USA

MEXICO

Gulf of Mexico

GALVESTON ISLAND

N

50 miles

50 km

Rivers and water features:
Sabine River
Sabine Lake
Neches River
Trinity River
Navasota River
Brazos River
Tenoxtitlán River
Mill Creek
San Marcos River
Colorado River
Cibolo River
Salado River
San Miguel River
Frio River
Nueces River
Hondo Creek
Rio Grande River
San Antonio River
Guadalupe River
La Baca River
Navidad River
Coleto Creek
Manahuilla Creek
Aransas River
San Jacinto River
Buffalo Bayou
Clear Creek
Dickson Creek
Chocolate Creek
Bastrop Creek
Oyster Creek
San Bernard River
Old Caney Creek
Peyton Creek
Raft Creek
Carancahua Creek
La Baca Bay
Matagorda Bay
Pass Cavallo
Espíritu Santo Bay
Aransas Pass
Corpus Christi Pass
Espíritu Santo Pass
West Pass
Point Bolivar
Galveston Bay

Places:
Jasper
Beaumont
Swartwout
Franklin
Liberty
Anahuac
Lynch's Ferry
New Washington
Harrisburg
Houston
Galveston
Quintana
Velasco
Brazoria
Columbia
Fort Bend
Richmond
Montgomery
Groce's Plantation
San Felipe de Austin
Washington-on-the-Brazos
La Grange
Columbus
Matagorda
Bastrop
Gonzales
Texana
Linville
Victoria
Lamar
Goliad
Presidio La Bahia (Fort Defiance)
Refugio
San Patricio
Fort Lipantitlán
Agua Dulce
Austin
Laredo
The Alamo
San Antonio de Béxar
Mission Concepción

The Opposing Sides

ORIGINS AND ORGANIZATION

Texian

On October 5, 1835, Major General Sam Houston made the following appeal from San Augustine for volunteers from the United States to rally to the defense of Texas:

> *War in defence of our Rights, our Oaths, and our Constitutions is inevitable in Texas!* If Volunteers from the United States will join their brethren in this section, they will receive liberal bounties of land. We have millions of acres of our best lands unchosen and unappropriated. Let each man come with a good rifle and one hundred rounds of ammunition – and come soon. Our war cry is "Liberty or Death." Our principles are to support the Constitution [of 1824], and *down with the Usurper*!!! (*CDLL*, October 13, 1835: 3:1)

Responding to the call, volunteers swelled the ranks of the military force being organized in Texas. Created on November 21, 1835, the Provisional Army was composed of: a small general staff; the Regular Army; the Permanent Volunteers; and the Auxiliary Volunteer Corps. The general staff consisted of the commander-in-chief, adjutant general, inspector general, quartermaster general, surgeon general, and four *aides-de-camp*. The Regular Army, which would serve after the Texas Revolution and be subject to the discipline and chain of command of the regular army of the United States, was composed of an infantry regiment and an artillery regiment, both consisting of 560 men. Each regiment was to have two battalions made up of five companies, each with 56 men. Field officers for the infantry regiment were to consist of a colonel, lieutenant colonel, and major. Each infantry company contained a captain and two lieutenants. The artillery regiment was officered by a colonel,

two lieutenant colonels, and two majors, with each artillery company led by a captain and three lieutenants. The infantry regiment was commanded by Colonel Edward Burleson, and the artillery regiment by Colonel James W. Fannin, Jr. A cavalry regiment was recruited during December 1835 composed of 384 men organized into five companies with Lieutenant Colonel William B. Travis in command.

Officers and privates of the Regular Army were subject to the same discipline and pay as in the regular army, and each noncommissioned officer and private was promised a bounty of 640 acres of land. Later, as an incentive to enlistment in the Regular Army, rather than with the volunteers, an additional bounty of 160 acres of land and $24 was offered; one-half of the money to be paid when the recruit reported at Army headquarters and the balance on the first quarterly payday thereafter.

Authorized on December 4, 1835, the Permanent Volunteers were enlisted for the duration of the Texas Revolution, and were permitted to elect their own officers. They were to receive the same pay, rations, and clothing as were allowed by the United States in the War of 1812 (1812–15), and, in addition, at the expiration of service, or when honorably discharged, were also to receive a bounty of 640 acres of land.

Also created was an Auxiliary Volunteer Corps of about 5,000 men who could enlist for from three to six months. These were mostly composed of recent emigrants or volunteer militia units from the United States. Those who served for six months were entitled to 320 acres of land, but those who served less time did not receive a bounty.

The majority of those who fought in the campaign of 1835 had been settled in Texas for some time. Most of them returned home to care for their families through the winter of 1835/36. As a consequence, many who fought in the campaign of 1836, which was over before the harvest released the veterans of the previous year for further service, were newcomers primarily from the southern United States.

Among these were two companies of New Orleans Greys, from Louisiana, commanded by Captain Thomas H. Breece and Captain Robert C. Morris, which later became known as the San Antonio Greys; the Red Rovers

ABOVE LEFT
This Broadside was produced in New Orleans on April 23, 1836, to encourage "settlers" to colonize Texas and fight Mexican attempts to seize back the newly established republic. (Broadside Collection, BC_0258, The Dolph Briscoe Center for American History, The University of Texas at Austin)

ABOVE RIGHT
The only flag believed to have been carried by the Texian army at San Jacinto was that of the Newport Volunteers, also known as the Buck Eye Rangers, initially recruited and commanded by Captain Sidney Sherman. Originally with a blue silk field, it shows a charging Lady Liberty with sword drawn and "Liberty or Death" emblazoned on a sash held on her sword. Recruited in Ohio and Kentucky in December 1835, the 52-man company was presented with the flag by the ladies of Newport, Kentucky, who had it painted by 22-year-old artist James H. Beard. When Sherman was elected to command the 2d Regt. Texas Volunteers in 1836, it was carried as a regimental flag. (Courtesy of the State Preservation Board, Austin, Texas; CHA #1989.068)

This plate depicts a volunteer from Captain William Blazeby's Infantry Company, formerly known as the New Orleans Greys, defending the Alamo against the Mexican attack. Having discharged his musket, he prepares to fend off a bayonet thrust as Mexican infantrymen scramble over the Alamo defenses.

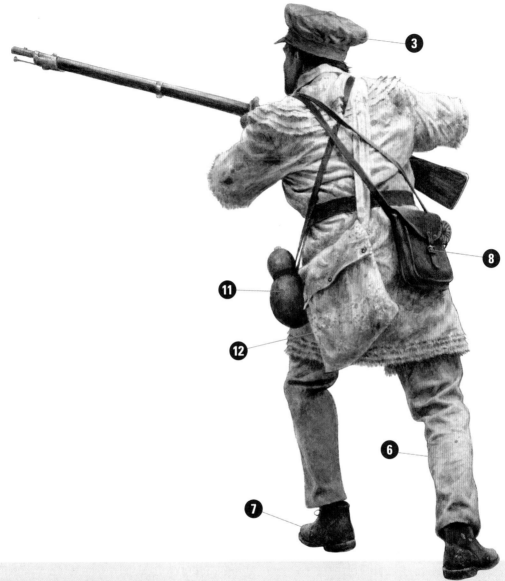

Weapons, dress, and equipment

His main weapon is a Model 1776 Charleville musket (**1**) with flintlock action. This fired a .69-caliber ball, and weighed 10lb. Its maximum range was about 100–200yd with an effective range of only about 50–75yd. The rate of fire of this weapon was two to three shots per minute in good hands. He also has a sailor's knife (**2**) with inlaid ivory handle in a vellum sheath attached to his leather waist belt via a stud on the reverse of the sheath pushed through a slit in the belt.

Headgear consists of a brown wool cap (**3**), with stiffened cardboard visor covered with same material, patterned after an 1825 military "chacos" or forage cap. His battle-scarred hunting coat (**4**) of unbleached tow linen is fastened by one pewter button at the neck, and hooks and eyes down the rest of the front. The coat has a double cape and collar, and fringes on the edges and seams. He wears a cotton checked shirt (**5**) under his coat. His fall-front trousers (**6**) are of white cotton duck. Footwear is a stout pair of russet leather brogans (**7**).

His accouterments consist of a crudely stitched leather ball pouch (**8**) filled with lead ball, extra flints, and leather wadding, suspended from a leather sling suspended over his left shoulder. A scrimshawed powder horn (**9**) is also hung from a narrow leather shoulder belt over his left shoulder. A brush and vent pick (**10**) for cleaning the firing mechanism of his musket are attached via a fine brass chain from his ball pouch shoulder strap. His water carrier (**11**) is a gourd suspended over his right shoulder via a narrow leather strap. Provisions are held in a cotton haversack (**12**) hung from the same shoulder.

and Mobile Greys, from Alabama, led by Dr. Jack Shackelford and Captain David N. Burke respectively; and the Mustangs, recruited in Bardstown, Kentucky, under Captain Burr H. Duval, all of which formed the Lafayette Battalion under Major Benjamin C. Wallace. Also the Georgia Battalion, commanded by Major William Ward, consisted of the Columbus Volunteers, Macon Volunteers, and Georgia Riflemen. To avoid increasing international tension between the United States and Mexico, most of these units were recruited with little publicity and, particularly in New Orleans, were described as "colonists" intent on settling in Texas.

Mexican

With about 130 generals and field-grade infantry commanders, the Mexican Army was overly supplied with officers, who were predominantly from the *criollo* classes (those of Spanish descent born in the colonies). These mainly consisted of veterans of the colonial army and of the War of Independence from Spain (1821), as well as numerous new political and social appointees. Within the latter, many were intellectually or temperamentally unsuited to command. Although used to privilege in civilian life, they lacked initiative in a military context, and some were negligent in their duties. In a report to the Chamber of Deputies on April 11, 1834, the Secretary of State and of the War Office, José Joaquín de Herrera, criticized the multitude of ranks and decorations conferred on those who did not know how to command troops, at the expense of many well-trained officers who retired from the service. This trend had a detrimental effect on the performance of some of the commanders of the Mexican army on the battlefields of Texas in 1836.

Others at the Alamo, such as General of Brigade Juan Valentin Amador, were brave and heroic in action. It was customary for junior lieutenants to be promoted from the experienced noncommissioned officers. Others could purchase a commission or receive the same via attendance and graduation from the *Colegio Militar* (Military Academy), originally established in 1824 in the fortress of San Carlos de Perote at Perote, Veracruz, and at Chapultepec Castle, in Mexico City, by 1833.

Most Mexican enlisted soldiers were of indigenous heritage, with a smaller number of *mestizos* (those of mixed ancestry). Volunteers were rare, and forced recruitment was the norm. On one occasion a recruiting officer wrote to his superior: "Here are 300 volunteers. I will send you 300 more if you return the chains" (quoted in Reston & Bach 1919: 9). Many conscripts were too old or too young, and some were released from local jails in return for military service. Once in the Army, however, these men made reasonable soldiers, being docile and relatively amenable to military instruction. They were smaller in stature at approximately 5ft 1in tall, as opposed to the average American who was 5ft 8in tall, but were used to hardship and were physically tough individuals.

Based on a drawing produced on the spot and published by Italian painter and lithographer Claudio Linati in *Civil, Military and Religious Costumes of Mexico* in 1828, this lithograph depicts General of Division Vicente Filisola, Santa Anna's second-in-command in 1836, wearing the undress uniform of a general of brigade. While a general of division wore a sky-blue silk sash around the waist, with two knots above the metallic gold fringes showing the same embroidery as on the coat, a general of brigade had a dark-green sash with one knot. Headgear consisted of a black bicorn hat edged with gold braid and white feathers, and topped with three loose green, white, and red plumes. (Courtesy Anne S.K. Brown Military Collection, Brown University, Providence)

Since Mexico's independence from Spain, the infantry of the Mexican Army had consisted of the *permanentes* (regular troops); the *activos* (active militia); and the *cívicos* (civic militia). Commanding the infantry was a cadre of generals supported by various staff officers. The cavalry, artillery, engineers, and *Zapadores* (sappers) were organized into their own separate branches of service, and there was a small medical corps.

Following the reduction in size of regiments from a two- to one-battalion organization in 1823, each infantry unit was designated a battalion. On November 19, 1833, the number of regular Infantry battalions was reduced from 12 to ten. Each battalion was commanded by a colonel or lieutenant colonel with staff composed of a chaplain, surgeon, armorer, sappers, drum major, and fifers. Also since 1833, each battalion consisted of six companies of fusiliers, one company of grenadiers, and one company of voltigeurs (sharpshooters). In December 1835, these battalions were reorganized and their numbered designations changed to names of distinguished leaders associated with the struggle for Mexican independence: Matamoros, Jiménez, Aldama, Morelos, Guerrero, Hidalgo, Allende, Abasolo, Galeana, and Landero. Only the first five named battalions served in the Texas campaign, and only the first three took part in the assault on the Alamo, Coleto Creek, and the defeat at San Jacinto. The other five remained on duty throughout the states of Mexico. Although the official strength of a regular battalion in the peacetime establishment was 823 and 1,223 on a war footing, the actual strength was always lower, varying from approximately 250 to 400 men during the campaign in Texas.

Inherited from the Spanish regime, active militia battalions were composed partly of embodied (full-time) troops on active duty, and a reserve made up of untrained recruits and conscripts. While later serving as Envoy Extraordinary and Minister Plenipotentiary to Mexico from February 1842 to March 1844, Waddy Thompson recalled seeing droves of "miserable and more than half naked wretches chained together and marching through the streets to the barracks" where they were "scoured and then dressed in a uniform made of linen cloth or of serge …"; he added they were "occasionally drilled," which consisted of mainly teaching them "to march in column through the streets" of Mexico City (Thompson 1846: 172–73).

Active militia units were organized like the regular troops and were known by the name of the city or state in which they were recruited. Although the battalions from San Luis Potosí, Toluca, Querétaro, Guanajuato, Mexico, Guadalajara, Tres Villas, and Yucatán took part in the Texas campaign, only the first two saw action at the Alamo, Coleto Creek,

Many Mexican officers wore wide-brimmed straw hats on campaign, as shown in this hand-colored engraving by William H. Dodd entitled "Equestrian portrait of General Santa Anna." Recalling the assault on the Alamo, 1st Lieutenant José Enrique de la Peña observed that he and a fellow officer donned white hats. Infantry officers in Mexico's Regular Army wore gold epaulets, while active militia officers were distinguished by silver epaulets. Colonels and lieutenant colonels wore a red silk waist sash; although they wore a bicorn hat with tricolor plume for gala dress, a shako was prescribed for active duty. (Brown Digital Repository, bdr:231283)

This plate depicts a fusilier of the Aldama Regular Infantry Battalion, 1st Infantry Brigade, Army of Operations against Texas. Having scaled a ladder thrown up against the Alamo defenses, he lunges with fixed bayonet at the nearest Texian defender waiting for him on the rampart.

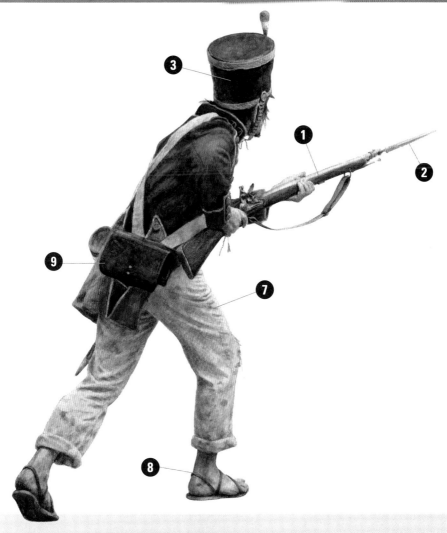

Weapons, dress, and equipment

He is armed with a .76-caliber 1809 India Pattern "Brown Bess" musket (**1**), with brown leather sling attached; its overall length is 55in and it weighs 9lb 11oz. It is sighted to 200yd with an accurate range of about 70yd. Attached to his musket is a triangular socket bayonet (**2**) with 17in blade and an Indian spring catch forged on, which prevented the bayonet from dropping off the end of the barrel.

His French-pattern shako (**3**) of black cowhide has yellow braided bands at top and bottom, and a patent-leather visor. A yellow loop with an "eagle and snake" button secures a cockade in Mexican national colors (**4**), beneath which is a brass cap plate and brass-scaled chinstrap. The cord and tassels normally attached to this shako were ordered to be removed before the assault on the Alamo. With broad scarlet lapels, his Turkish blue tailcoat (**5**) is of the pattern produced via the 1832 clothing contract. The letters "BA," representing *Batallon Aladama*, are embroidered in yellow thread on either side of his collar (**6**). His tattered fall-front trousers (**7**) are of white cotton. Like many of his comrades, he wears leather sandals (**8**) as his shoes were worn out during the forced march to the Alamo.

His accouterments consist of a black leather cartridge pouch (**9**), attached to a whitened buff leather belt over his left shoulder, containing a pine block drilled with holes to accommodate cartridges. Mexican troops were seldom issued with more than two or three rounds at a time so these blocks were rarely full. A brass-mounted leather bayonet scabbard (**10**) is carried in a frog on a belt over his right shoulder. A brush and vent pick (**11**) are suspended from the "eagle and snake" plate attached to this belt. Suspended from a narrow leather carrying strap, his wooden, keg-shaped water-bottle (**12**) with cork stopper holds about one quart of water. His knapsack has been left behind Mexican lines. A dark-blue overcoat of Querétaro cloth with yellow-metal buttons was prescribed for winter wear, but this was seldom issued to troops involved in the campaign of 1836 despite the harsh winter conditions experienced during the march north.

and San Jacinto. Having seen action in the wars between the Centralists and Federalists in 1832 and 1835, some active militia battalions were by now veteran units.

As with the infantry, the regular cavalry was reorganized in 1835 and given names as opposed to numbered designations: the 1st and 8th regiments were amalgamated into the Tampico Regiment; the 2d, 7th, and Active regiments of Mexico became the Palmar Regiment; the 3d and 6th regiments became the Dolores Regiment; the 4th and 10th regiments became the Iguala Regiment; the 5th and 9th regiments became the Vera Cruz Regiment; and the 11th and 12th regiments became the Cuautla Regiment. The Yucatán Squadron and Tampico Company remained unchanged.

Organized in 1822, the civic militia was the basic reserve and citizens' militia of Mexico. Any Mexican male able to bear arms and aged 18 through 40 could be enlisted. On paper these units consisted of volunteers, but in reality their ranks were filled by choosing one man in every 100 who would be required occasionally to attend drill instruction, and they could be ordered into military service in the event of emergencies. This branch of service was virtually nonexistent, however, after Santa Anna ruthlessly quelled a revolt in Zacatecas in May 1835, caused when he questioned the right of a state to support a militia. As a result, he was forced to build his army around the regular troops and active militia.

TRAINING AND TACTICS

Texian

While a number of seasoned frontiersmen in the mold of David Crockett rallied to the cause of Texas Independence, many others were farmers,

BELOW LEFT
Based on a photograph by Samuel B. Hill of an earlier engraving, this portrait of Colonel James Bowie, who commanded the Texian infantry at the Alamo, was published by Charles M. Barnes in *Combats and Conquests of Immortal Heroes* in 1910. (Internet Archive)

BELOW RIGHT
This portrait of David Crockett by Chester Harding was painted in 1834 while he was in Boston, Massachusetts, promoting his autobiography. (National Portrait Gallery, Smithsonian Institution, NPG.2021.2)

tradesmen, and artisans whose backgrounds ranged from the wealthiest professional to the impoverished tradesman or laborer. Some, like lawyer Daniel W. Cloud and teacher Micajah Autry, were well educated, while others, such as flatboatman Robert Cunningham and plasterer Andrew Duvalt, were likely only semiliterate. Although some had experience fighting Native Americans, most of these men had received little formal military training other than the occasional attendance at militia musters in their home state.

On December 6, 1835, Major General Houston sent two agents, along with the commissioners, to the United States to purchase among other supplies 26 copies of Crop's *Discipline and Regulations,* which was probably a republication of *Regulations for the Order and Discipline of the Troops of the United States,* a drill manual written by Inspector General Friedrich Wilhelm von Steuben during the American Revolutionary War (1775–83) and still in use during the War of 1812. Also required were 100 copies of Scott's *Infantry Drill,* which was likely *Infantry Tactics; or, Rules for the Exercise and Manoeuvres of the Infantry of the U.S. Army,* by Major General Winfield Scott, published in 1825, and 36 copies of McComb's *School of the Soldier,* which was probably another reference to Scott's *Infantry Tactics,* as advocated by Alexander Macomb, Commanding General of the US Army 1828–41. It is not known whether these drill books were acquired, nor to what extent it may have been possible to use them given the great variety of arms carried by the Texians.

Mexican

As the training of infantry recruits was undertaken within the ranks, rather than at training depots, there were many poorly trained men present within a battalion. As a result, about one-third of the personnel of the five battalions in action at the Alamo were new recruits, and many were so inexperienced that General of Division Santa Anna ordered that they be kept out of the assault columns. According to Waddy Thompson:

> Their military bands are good, and the men learn to march indifferently well – they put their feet down as if they were feeling for the place, and do not step with that jaunty, erect and graceful air which is so beautiful in well drilled troops. As to the wheelings of well-trained troops, like the opening and shutting of a gate, or the prompt and exact execution of other evolutions, they know nothing about them. (Thompson 1846: 172–73)

Published in Spain in 1836 in *Prontuario Manual de Infanteria para la instruccion de los cuerpos de la Guardia Nacional* ("Infantry Manual for the Instruction of the Corps of the National Guard"), these engravings illustrate some of the orders given by Mexican Army officers signaling with wooden batons and canes at that time. The orders given from top to bottom are "Regular step," "Order for Guides or Markers," and "Attend Mass." Carried as a mark of rank by Mexican colonels, lieutenant colonels, and adjutants, canes were often employed to beat recalcitrant soldiers and maintain discipline in battle. (Internet Archive)

Following independence from Spain, Mexican officials changed title pages but otherwise adopted Spanish drill manuals and tactics of 1821. That used by Mexican infantry in 1836 was the *Reglamento para el Ejercicio y Maniobras de la Infanteria: mandado observar en la Republica Mexicana* ("Regulation for the Exercise and Maneuvers of the Infantry: ordered to be observed in the Mexican Republic"), published in 1829.

Although providing instruction for pre-1835 regimental-sized units, commanders could still apply the contents of the manuals at battalion level. They provided detailed drill instruction for the training of the individual

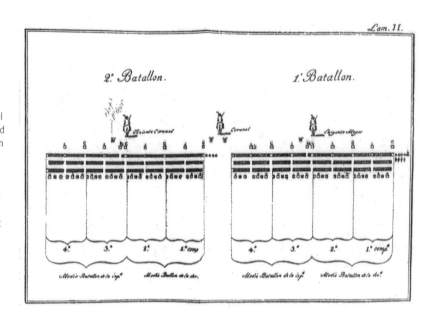

Showing a regiment of two battalions in parade order, Plate 2 of the *Reglamento para el Ejercicio y Maniobras de la Infanteria: mandado observar en la Republica Mexicana* still provided drill instruction at regimental level because the volume continued in use after the reorganization of Mexican infantry into battalion-sized units in 1835. The colonel stands eight paces ahead of the front rank with the lieutenant colonel and sergeant major to his left and right respectively. The captains, senior lieutenants, and flag-bearers form a line four paces ahead of the front rank. The drummers and bandsmen stand in two rows on the right flank of their battalions. Each company formed three files with a gap of two paces between each file. (Internet Archive)

soldier, and for the maneuver of the company and battalion, plus orders issued via drum and fife. It was a complicated system of instruction, however, and consequently it could be performed effectively only by veteran infantrymen within the regular battalions. As a result, training for the active militia was less complicated, with recruits or conscripts drilled to march in simple column formation and dress ranks on the firing line.

Published in the same year was the *Manual de guias para la instruccion de los sargentos de infanteria* ("Manual of Guidelines for the Training of Infantry Sergeants"), published by S. Perez, Calle de Angel, Mexico City. Again based on the tactics of 1821, this volume provided noncommissioned officers with a complete guide for training the enlisted infantryman to use, clean, and maintain the musket, plus the duties of the guard and sentinel soldier.

The cavalry branch of service employed the two-volume *Reglamento para el Ejercicio y Maniobras de la Caballería* ("Regulations for the Exercise and Maneuvers of the Cavalry"), published by the Royal Press in Madrid, Spain, in 1825. The trooper was trained and drilled on foot and horseback, and

From left to right, these antiquated figures from the *Reglamento para el Ejercicio y Maniobras de la Infanteria: mandado observar en la Republica Mexicana* of 1829 show a *soldado* at "support – arms;" "present – arms;" "charge – musket;" "prepare to fire;" and "take aim." (Internet Archive)

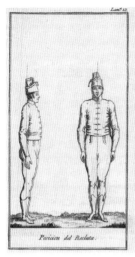

Three plates from the *Reglamento para el Ejercicio y Maniobras de la Caballería* of 1825 illustrate the training of cavalry recruits. After dismounted drill, recruits were taught to mount and ride their horse bareback before being given a saddle. (Internet Archive)

in how to maintain his weapons, equipage, and horse equipment. This was followed by company, squadron, and regimental instruction.

Regarding the civic militia, their organization, salary, ranks, uniform, and armament were outlined in the *Reglamento Para La Milicia Civica del Estado de Coahuila y Texas* ("Regulations for the Civil Militia of the State of Coahuila and Mexico"), published in Monclova, Mexico, in 1834.

In battle, the main tactic most Mexican infantrymen were expected to perform was the frontal attack. While a veteran soldier might be capable of loading and firing two rounds per minute, live-round musketry practice was virtually nonexistent, and the Mexican recruit's first experience of firing a musket was at his first battle. In general, he was forced to overload his musket to compensate for the notoriously poor-quality gunpowder that contained too much sulfur and charcoal. To protect himself from the resulting heavy recoil of his weapon, he often fired from the hip, thus causing the musket ball to fly on a high trajectory well over the heads of the enemy. As a result, Mexican commanders tended to place more faith in the bayonet charge in battle.

UNIFORMS AND WEAPONS

Texian

The clothing of the Texians at the outset of the fighting in 1835 was that of the civilian, with some wearing the deerskin of the frontiersman. Elected a lieutenant when the Gonzales militia was formed in October of that year, Valentine Bennett stated that nine out of ten Texians were in rags. With James Bowie and James Fannin, Jr. at the battle of Mission Concepción on October 27, 1835, Texian volunteer Noah Smithwick described the appearance of his comrades, writing:

> Buckskin breeches were the nearest approach to uniform, and there was wide diversity
> even there, some being new and soft and yellow, while others, from long familiarity
> with rain and grease and dirt, had become hard and black and shiny. Some, from

having passed through the process of wetting and drying on the wearer while he sat on the ground or a chunk before the camp fire, with his knees elevated at an angle of eighty-five degrees, had assumed an advanced position at the knee, followed by a corresponding shortening of the lower front length … Boots being an unknown quantity; some wore shoes and some moccasins. Here a broad-brimmed sombrero overshadowed the military cap at its side; there a tall "begum" rode familiarly beside a coonskin cap, with the tail hanging down behind … In lieu of a canteen, each man carried a Spanish gourd, a curious specimen of the gourd family, having two round bowls, each holding near a quart, connected by a short neck, apparently designed for adjusting a strap about. A fantastic military array to a casual observer, but the one great purpose animating every heart clothed us in a uniform more perfect in our eyes than was ever donned by regulars on dress parade. (Smithwick 1900: 109–10)

Regarding the clothing of Texian commanders, for many years after the Alamo, Private Felix Nuñez, who took part in the assault on the south wall and main gate of the fort on March 6, 1836, secretly kept the coat worn by Lieutenant Colonel William B. Travis, which he described as "'home-made' of Texas jeans" (SADE, June 30, 1889: 3:3). Surviving the battle at Coleto Creek 23 days later, Joseph H. Spohn, of the Alabama Red Rovers, later recalled that when executed at Goliad by Mexican firing squad, Colonel Fannin wore an "overcoat … of India rubber" and that his "bloody cap" lay in a pile with other clothing after the executions (ES, July 28, 1836: 2:2).

Arriving in Texas during November 1835, the two companies of the New Orleans Greys were the first volunteers joining the Texian Army to wear a semblance of uniform. The First Company was referred to as the Volunteer Greys in the New Orleans press as early as October 19, 1835 (NOB, October 19, 1835, 2:1). According to Private Herman Ehrenberg, a young German immigrant who joined its ranks: "We all quickly purchased ourselves clothing, grey in color, suitable for life in the prairie, which we found ready made in the numerous stores, from which the name of our company was derived" (Ehrenberg 1843: 11–12). After reaching Nacogdoches, Texas, an unknown member of the First Company wrote on November 9, 1835: "we have now quite a military appearance, – we have shoulder pieces made of wool, with silver plated scales on our caps, [plus] canteens, flasks and pistols …" (NOCB, November 27, 1835: 2:2). Ebenezer Heath, a member of the Second Company, wrote on March 10, 1836: "The color of our uniform was a grey jacket and pants with a sealskin cap. We arrived with rifles, pistols, swords and large knives" (Davenport Papers).

Recruited mainly in and around Courtland, Alabama, during December 1835, the Red Rovers wore coonskin caps and were clothed by local womenfolk in "linsey-woolsey" fringed hunting shirts with bright red, green, and brown checks, and jean trousers dyed bright red. They also carried a simple red banner as their company flag (Talley 2002: 21). The Red Rovers were issued with Model 1830 US Cadet Muskets loaned from the state arsenal at Mount Vernon (Elliott 1947: 322).

By the beginning of 1836, some clothing and military equipment was received by the Texian Army. On January 28, a shipment of supplies was sent from New Orleans via several vessels by Texas purchasing agent Edward Hall. Clothing included 360 jackets, 360 pairs of pantaloons, 744 shirts, 12

Based on a full-length painting of David Crockett produced in 1834 by John C. Chapman but destroyed by fire in 1881, this hand-colored mezzotint shows the famous frontiersman dressed in hunting shirt, buckskin leggings, and moccasins, with a Kentucky rifle and hunting dogs. Crockett fought and died in the ranks of the Tennessee Mounted Volunteers at the Alamo. (National Portrait Gallery, Smithsonian Institution, S/NPG.99.171)

red flannel shirts, 12 gingham twilled shirts, 400 russet brogans, and 1,200 men's untanned brogans. Equipment consisted of 200 cartridge boxes and belts, and 432 canteens. That some of this clothing was received and issued to Texian volunteers is evidenced by a receipt issued during the next month by Jones M. Townsend to Governor Henry Smith at San Felipe for two jersey round jackets, three pairs of satinet pants, and 23 pairs of brogans (Jenkins 1973: 4.167 & 4.297).

Nevertheless, on March 10, 1836, Captain John S. Brooks, an adjutant under Fannin's command at Goliad, wrote: "I have neither clothes nor money to buy them. The Government furnishes us with nothing, - not even ammunition" (Readings in Texas History: 291). Reminiscing in 1895 about his participation in the battle of San Jacinto, James M. Hill, who served in Co. H, 1st Regt. Texian Volunteers, stated: "I wore then like all the others citizens clothes. I also wore a fur cap ..." (quoted in McArdle 1895: n.p.).

In order that Texians might differentiate between Mexican troops and the *Tejanos* in Captain Juan N. Seguín's cavalry company at San Jacinto, Houston originally ordered them to remain in Harrisburg to guard the sick. Following protests from Seguín, the order was rescinded and playing cards were distributed to the *Tejanos*, which they wore in their hats to identify them as Texian soldiers.

Dr. Joseph H. Bernard, a surgeon with Fannin, commented that the Texians were "abundantly supplied with provisions, and with arms and ammunition, and almost every man had his rifle and brace of pistols, besides there were a number of good English muskets captured from the Mexicans …" (quoted in Wooton 1898: 615). The Second Company of New Orleans Greys, commanded by Captain Robert C. Morris, brought with them an 18-pounder cannon that was dragged about 200 miles from Velasco, on the Texas coast, to San Antonio de Béxar, arriving two days after General of Brigade Martin Perfecto de Cos surrendered. Their cannon was subsequently installed in the Alamo defenses.

Mexican

As a result of the 1832 clothing contract, both regular and militia infantrymen wore a dress uniform consisting of a tailcoat of *azul turqui* (Turkish blue), cloth predominantly produced in the city of Querétaro, a major center for the Mexican textile industry, with collar, broad lapels and turnbacks of scarlet with white piping, and yellow-metal "eagle and snake" buttons. In 1835, unit numbers embroidered on either side of the collar were changed to letters.

Full-dress headgear consisted of a French-pattern shako of stiffened cowhide with brass plate and chinstrap, cotton cords, and an elongated tricolor wool pompon. For full dress, elite companies wore *hombreros* (shoulder pads), which were red for grenadiers, green for voltigeurs, and dark blue piped with scarlet for fusiliers.

Still in production 15 months later, tailcoats supplied with the contract uniform were changed in June 1833 to dark blue trimmed with red collar, cuffs, and piping, but minus broad red lapels, partially based on a pattern originally prescribed in 1821. Dark-blue cloth, as well as white, pantaloons appear to have been issued. As a result, both 1832- and 1833-pattern uniforms were in use during the Texas campaign, with the earlier pattern being worn mostly by the active militia.

In 1834, the regulations concerning the civil militia of the state of Coahuila and Texas prescribed a dark-blue coat with bright-red collar and cuffs; yellow was to be worn as a facing color if red was not available. Buttons were brass, trousers were dark blue, and headgear was to consist of a leather helmet or hat (Chartrand 1996: 15).

For regular line cavalry, the 1832 clothing contract provided a tailcoat of scarlet Querétaro cloth with dark-green collar, lapels, and cuffs, with coarse lining and white-metal "eagle and serpent" buttons. Also of Querétaro cloth, dark-

Entitled "Soldier in undress," this Linati lithograph shows a Mexican infantryman in white warm-weather cloth or canvas jacket and pants, and shako with white cloth cover. Although the 1832 clothing contract did not include pantaloons, it did supply each man with an undress uniform consisting of two white cloth or canvas jackets and trousers with plain white-metal buttons, two linen shirts, two velveteen neckties, two pairs of shoes, and one dark-blue barracks cap with red band, tassel, and visor. (Courtesy Anne S.K. Brown Military Collection, Brown University, Providence)

blue trousers had an antelope-skin seat lining and scarlet stripe on the outer seams, and were worn over half-boots. Dragoon-pattern helmets of stiffened black leather had a brass "eagle and snake" plate, crest, and chin scales, with black goat-hair comb and pompon. The regimental number was worn on the white-metal buttons and collar. As with the infantry, 1832-pattern tailcoats for cavalry were changed in 1833 to scarlet with green trim but minus broad green lapels, based on an earlier pattern prescribed in 1824. Thus, both 1832- and 1833-pattern coats were likely in use during the Texas campaign.

Since 1824, active militia cavalry regiments had worn green tailcoats with scarlet collar, cuffs, and turnbacks, with scarlet edging on the rest of the coat, and white-metal buttons. Other items were as for the regular line cavalry. Both regular and militia cavalry also had a white cotton jacket and trousers for warm weather, and a fatigue cap.

Formed as a corps in 1827, Mexican artillery wore uniforms similar to the infantry, being described in an earlier undated circular as "a dark blue coat with scarlet collar, cuffs and piping, black velvet lapels with silver buttonhole lace" (*AHM*, XI/481.3/155). As the artillery traditionally used gold and yellow buttons and lace, it is probable silver was never worn and this was changed to yellow metal and gold lace soon after. The waistcoat and trousers were white.

Created as a corps in 1822, the Engineers and Battalion of Sappers wore uniforms similar to those of the artillery, with collar and lapels edged with silver for officers and white for sappers. Officers' buttons were silver while those of sappers were of white metal. Sappers may also have worn silver or white "castle turrets" embroidered on the collar (Chartrand 1996: 14). Some sappers traditionally carried axes, along with other sidearms, with which to clear obstructions and smash through enemy defenses in the path of the army.

Infantry weapons consisted of the .76-caliber Third Model 1809 India Pattern "Brown Bess" musket made by Ezekiel Baker, with an effective range of about 100yd. Condemned as unserviceable by the British Government, these weapons were purchased by Mexico during the 1830–40 period. Some infantry and mounted men carried shorter shotguns with Spanish

The Mexican regular cavalry officer in this Linati lithograph wears the 1824-pattern uniform, which was reintroduced in 1833. His scarlet coat has green facings on the collar and pointed cuffs with an embroidered palm-leaf badge on the former and elaborate trim on the latter. His helmet has a black comb with brass crescent, plate, and scale chinstrap. The trooper in the background wears the yellow cloak issued for cold-weather service. (Courtesy Anne S.K. Brown Military Collection, Brown University, Providence)

The warm-weather dress of the Active Militia Cavalry of Guazacualco, south of Veracruz, included white cotton jackets. Both Active Militia cavalry and Presidial Permanent cavalry carried lances, sabers, and carbines. (Courtesy Anne S.K. Brown Military Collection, Brown University, Providence)

Miguelet locks, with the mechanism in front of the lock plate. Sergeants and corporals also carried a flat-bladed and slightly curved *sabre-briquet* or French Napoleonic short sword, also known as a hanger, in a double frog with the bayonet.

Weapons carried by regular line and active militia cavalry consisted of the saber, pistol, and the *tercerola*, or carbine. The carbines were possibly Baker models of the same caliber as the muskets, and weighed 6.5lb with an overall length of 36in. The sight was fixed and the muzzle had a deep funnel to hold ball and patch while the ramrod was being drawn by the mounted cavalryman.

Carried by regular and Presidial cavalry, the lance was about 9ft in overall length with a shaft of either beech or hazel wood. Attached below its metal tip was a fork-tailed *banderole* (pennant). Apart from decoration, this served to scare the enemy's horses when they saw it fluttering immediately before their eyes in battle. The lance was steadied in the lancer's grip by a leather strap secured to the shaft. When not used in action, the end of the lance was placed in a socket attached to his right-hand stirrup.

The Alamo

March 6, 1836

BACKGROUND TO BATTLE

News of an armed uprising at Gonzales reached Santa Anna on October 23, 1835. Determined to crush the revolt, he transferred his presidential duties to Miguel Barragán on a temporary basis in order to lead troops into Texas personally. Santa Anna believed the rebels would be quickly cowed, a view not shared by his Italian-born deputy commander, General of Division Vicente Filisola. As there were only about 2,500 soldiers available within the Mexican interior, and these were needed to crush revolts in Jalisco, Nuevo Leon, San Luis, and Zacatecas, Santa Anna began to assemble a new army at San Luis Potosí, which he named the "Army of Operations against Texas."

At Santa Anna's behest, on December 30, 1835, the Mexican Congress passed the Tornel Decree, which declared that any foreigners fighting against Mexican troops would be "deemed pirates and dealt with as such, being citizens of no nation presently at war with the Republic and fighting under no recognized flag" (*DRT* 1836). In the early 19th century, captured pirates were executed immediately, so the resolution thus gave the Mexican Army permission to take no prisoners in the war against the Texians. This information was not widely distributed, and it is unlikely that most of the American volunteers serving in the Texian Army were aware that there would be no prisoners-of-war.

The march of Santa Anna's Army of Operations from San Luis Potosí to Presidio del Rio Grande, also known as Guerrero, via Saltillo, Monclova, and Laredo, crossed about 500 miles of mountainous terrain and desert. The First Division, commanded by General of Brigade Joaquin Ramirez y Sesma, set off on December 10, 1835, and reached Laredo 16 days later. There Sesma found the remnants of Cos's command; according to Filisola, they were one of "the worst fed, clothed, shod, armed and mounted" units, being largely composed of the convicts and raw recruits that had reinforced Cos on December 8, 1835 (Filisola 1848–49: 2.271).

The 1st Infantry Brigade of the Second Division, under Brevet General of Brigade Antonio Gaona, marched north from San Luis Potosí on December 22, followed two days later by the 2d Infantry Brigade, led by General of Brigade Eugenio Tolsa, and four days after that by the Cavalry Brigade, commanded by General of Brigade Juan José Andrade. By January 5, 1836, the entire Second Division, plus the Cavalry Brigade, was concentrated at Saltillo, where the raw troops received their first military instruction and training.

The columns were accompanied by 1,000 pack mules, 33 four-wheeled wagons, and 200 two-wheeled carts, plus a large number of camp followers. On arrival at Saltillo, Santa Anna was stricken with a stomach ailment that laid him low for about two weeks. The march was undertaken during winter with troops clothed in summer uniforms and ill-equipped for such conditions. During some days, heavy snow settled to a depth of 15–16in and up to the knees of the troops. On others, the extreme dry cold led to at least 32 men, women, and children dying from a lack of water (Filisola 1848–49: 2.277). Despite this, the bulk of the army made good time, averaging 15–20 miles per day.

This "flaming bomb" insignia was excavated near Saltillo on the route of one of Santa Anna's marches into Texas. It was attached to the shakos worn by the grenadiers of a Mexican infantry battalion, plus the personnel of the Sapper Battalion. The reverse view shows how the insignia was secured to the headgear via a metal prong. (Adam Ochs Fleischer collection)

While re-supplying his troops at Presidio del Rio Grande, Santa Anna learned that the Texians proposed to occupy Matamoros, and directed General of Brigade José de Urrea to march 250 men southeast to Matamoros with orders to link up with a battalion approaching north from Yucatán. Urrea would then march north along the Atascocita Road and across the Rio Grande River protecting the right flank of the main army. Also while at Presidio del Rio Grande, Santa Anna decided to reorganize his field army, so that the former First Division became the Vanguard Brigade, while the Second Division was dissolved and the rest of the main body of the "Army of Operations against Texas" was now composed of three infantry brigades and one cavalry brigade. Urrea's smaller column, initially designated the Independent Brigade, was later expanded into a division. The Mexican force totaled about 6,100 men with 21 pieces of artillery. Continuing its march north across the desert, the reorganized army found the prairies had been fired and the grass burned. Also, several soldiers were killed by marauding Comanches who staged ambushes when they could.

Meanwhile, the advancing Mexican army went largely unnoticed by the Texians, some of whom distrusted reports of its approach made by their *Tejano* scouts. Owing to recruitment and fundraising in the United States, their army had begun to grow in size again, reaching about 1,000 men by the end of January 1836. At least half of them, however, were involved in the Matamoros Expedition led by colonels Fannin, James Grant, and Frank W. Johnson, who were at odds with each other about who should command as they gathered men at Refugio.

At San Antonio de Béxar, Lieutenant Colonel James C. Neill commanded the battered defenses in the Alamo Mission, which were in poor condition.

Joined by Bowie and his company of 19 men in mid-January, the Alamo garrison amounted to only about 115–20 men, which was perhaps one-sixth of the number required to hold the place. Despite this, Neill believed that holding the Alamo was vital to the defense of Texas as it lay on the main overland invasion route from Mexico, and was the only settlement of any consequence in southern Texas. Nicknamed "Benito" by Bowie, Major Green B. Jameson was appointed chief engineer of the Texian forces at the Alamo on February 11, 1836, and was given responsibility for coordinating the work to improve the defenses.

Lieutenant Colonel Travis arrived at the post with a company of about 30 mounted men, including eight *Tejanos*, on or about February 3, with orders from Governor Smith to take command. The arrival of Travis created a problem: officially both he and Neill were now in joint command as Smith had neglected to relieve the latter upon appointing Travis. Bowie outranked them both, however. This situation was partially resolved when Neill left on a 20-day furlough as a result of ill-health in his family on February 13, but difficulties soon arose between Travis and Bowie, and between Travis and the men of the garrison, most of whom rejected the discipline he was attempting to impose on them. To resolve the matter, an election was called by Travis, and Bowie was almost unanimously chosen as commander of the volunteers, which left Travis with only about 30 regulars under his command. In the end, the two men reached a compromise and Travis took charge of the cavalry, while Bowie commanded the infantry at the Alamo. As Bowie became increasingly unwell with typhoid fever, Travis assumed overall command.

During the following days, both men signed numerous letters requesting more men and supplies, but little was forthcoming, although the 15-strong Tennessee Mounted Volunteers, led by Captain William B. Harrison, and including David Crockett, joined them on February 8.

On February 16, *Tejano* supporter of the revolution Ambrosio Rodrigues sent Travis a message reporting that Santa Anna's army was about to cross the Rio Grande, and urging him to abandon the Alamo and fall back to the army that Houston was forming at Gonzales. Four days later a messenger, another *Tejano*, arrived from Blas Herrera with news that about 5,000 Mexican troops had crossed the Rio Grande several days earlier. By this time, Santa Anna had reached Hondo Creek, less than 50 miles from San Antonio de Béxar. Although some of the Texian officers doubted the accuracy of these reports, Travis was inclined to believe them, and determined to continue strengthening the Alamo defenses while posting a lookout in the tower of the San Fernando Cathedral. He also sent yet another dispatch to Smith pleading for reinforcements.

On February 21, the lead echelon of Santa Anna's troops reached the Medina River, only 25 miles from San Antonio de Béxar. Santa Anna ordered Sesma to organize a cavalry force to make a surprise strike in order to catch the Texians off-guard. Fate intervened, however, when sudden heavy rain raised the level of the Medina, preventing the Mexican cavalry from crossing the river.

Santa Anna's troops arrived at San Antonio de Béxar on the morning of February 23. As the Texians and *Tejanos* made their final withdrawal into

The standard weapon for Mexican infantrymen was the .75-caliber 1809 India Pattern lower "Brown Bess" musket. Considered unserviceable and surplus to requirements by the British Government, approximately 100,000 of these weapons were purchased by Mexico via loans made by the merchant banking house of Barclay, Herring, Richardson & Company, of London. (NMAH Acc. No. 319944)

the Alamo, Travis sent another courier with a plea for help "To the People of Texas & All Americans in the World …" (Travis 1836: 1). Soon after the first elements of the Mexican army, consisting of the Vanguard Battalion, entered San Antonio de Béxar, they raised a "blood red flag" from the tower of the San Fernando Cathedral, which indicated "no quarter." In response, the Texians fired a defiant cannon shot. On the same day, James B. Bonham arrived back at the Alamo after his attempt to get help and reinforcements from Fannin, the commander at Goliad.

Early on February 24, a gravely sick Bowie handed complete command of the Alamo defenses to Travis. Eight Mexican siege guns opened up on the Alamo that afternoon and courier Albert Martin slipped through the incomplete Mexican lines carrying a letter from Travis to Gonzales and beyond, which stated, "I am besieged."

On February 25, about 300 Mexican infantry occupied La Villita, which was only about 100yd from the walls of the Alamo. A party of Texians sallied out to burn some of the *jacales* (huts), which offered the Mexicans cover. Although initially driven back with two killed, the Mexicans returned later that day and dug in. That night, Mexican sappers dug more trenches that were quickly occupied by the Matamoros Regular Infantry Battalion, while two more batteries were established, one about 300yd south of the Alamo and the other near an old Powder House, about 1,000yd to the southeast. This effectively meant the Alamo was under siege from three sides, with only the northern approaches remaining open.

On February 27, Santa Anna ordered the bombardment of the Alamo to commence. The Mexicans were unable to seal off the irrigation ditch supplying the fort with water, while Bonham slipped out to the north carrying yet another desperate message to Fannin. Behind the Mexican lines, Santa Anna sent a courier to Mexico City announcing that San Antonio de Béxar had been captured, but failed to mention the resistance he still faced in the Alamo. Farther north at Gonzales, the Ranging Company of Mounted

Volunteers set out under Lieutenant George C. Kimball to reinforce the Alamo garrison.

Meanwhile, on February 28 a relief expedition led by Fannin finally set out for the Alamo, leaving a company of regulars to defend Fort Defiance. Realizing their plan was impracticable in the face of Mexican superior numbers, however, Fannin and his command swiftly returned to the fort. Also on February 28, the Mexicans again tried to cut off the water supply to the Alamo, and established an artillery battery at the Old Mill, 800yd north of the mission. The next day, Bonham again reached Goliad, where Fannin informed him that he was unable to send relief.

On March 1, the Gonzales Ranging Company rode into the Alamo. All remained quiet until March 3, when Bonham returned with a message from Major Robert M. Williamson urging Travis to hold out and promising that help was on the way. Within the Mexican lines, more reinforcements gave Santa Anna a total of 2,400 men and ten pieces of artillery. On March 4, the newly arrived guns were established in battery only 220yd from the north wall of the Alamo. Later that day, Santa Anna held a meeting with his senior officers to discuss whether an attempt should be made to take the Alamo by storm.

Amid obvious signs that the Mexicans were about to make their final assault, Travis called the Alamo garrison together that evening and delivered a passionate speech. Although there is no evidence that he drew a line in the sand with his sword over which those who agreed to stay and fight would cross, he is believed to have offered each man a choice between fighting to the death and attempting to escape. During that same evening it was agreed that Seguín and two of his men should ride out and hasten to Goliad once again, and ask Fannin to reinforce them at the Alamo. A Mexican woman also slipped out and into Santa Anna's lines to report on the desperate state of the defenders.

On March 5, Santa Anna determined that the time had come to storm the Alamo, and by mid-afternoon he had formulated his battle plan. Only seasoned troops were to be involved in the action, while all untrained volunteers and conscripts, involving about 315 men, were to remain in camp.

The first column, consisting of 200 fusiliers and voltigeurs of the Aldama Regular Battalion and 100 fusiliers from the San Luis Potosí Active Militia Battalion, under the command of Cos, would attack the northwest corner of the fort. They would carry ten ladders, two crowbars, and two axes.

A second column, consisting of about 400 men under Colonel Francisco Duque and composed of the Toluca Active Militia Battalion, minus grenadiers, and three fusilier companies of the San Luis Potosí Active Militia Battalion, carrying the same number of ladders, crowbars, and axes, would attack the north wall.

A third column, led by Colonel José Maria Romero and composed of 400 fusiliers of the Matamoros and Jiménez Regular Infantry battalions, carrying six ladders, would attack from the east in the vicinity of the corral.

A fourth column under Colonel Juan Morales and made up of three voltigeur companies from the Matamoros, Jiménez, and San Luis Potosí battalions, carrying two ladders, would attack the south side of the fort

and attempt to break through the *abatis* and palisade wall linking it to the chapel. To the east of the fort, a squadron of lancers from the Dolores Regular Cavalry Regiment would cut off the retreat of any Texians during the assault.

The reserve was composed of 385 men and consisted of 200 grenadiers from the Matamoros, Jiménez, Aldama, Toluca, and San Luis Potosí battalions, and 185 men from the Sapper Battalion. Meanwhile, 380 cavalrymen, under Sesma, were to patrol the surrounding countryside to prevent further Texian reinforcements from reaching the Alamo during the assault. The Mexican artillery would remain silent throughout the assault in order to avoid inflicting casualties on their own troops.

In order that his assault troops could rest before the assault, Santa Anna ordered that all fire should cease at 2200hrs on March 5. He ordered the militiamen of the Toluca and San Luis Potosí battalions to dig a new approach trench about halfway between the existing lines north of the Alamo and the fort itself. Around 1700hrs the Mexican reserve force began moving into position. Inside the Alamo, the defenders took advantage of the lull to repair what they could of the defenses, and then snatch some rest. In a last attempt to secure help, 21-year-old James Allen rode out of the fort under cover of darkness.

At midnight, the Mexican officers and NCOs began to awaken their soldiers. At 0100hrs on March 6, the four Mexican assault columns began to move into their assigned positions, which they had reached by 0400hrs. Each was about 250yd from the walls of the Alamo. Once in position, the attack troops were ordered to lie down and rest. Despite the fact that Travis had posted three men between the walls of the Alamo and the Mexican lines as pickets, none raised the alarm. Santa Anna and his staff took up position by the battery to the north of the fort.

This photograph of a painting entitled "Siege of the Alamo" by San Antonio resident Professor L.R. Bromley was produced in 1884. The original, described at the time in the *Dallas Daily Herald* as the "most wonderful art work ever exhibited in the south," was on exhibition at the Star Art Gallery in Dallas, Texas. The location of the original painting is unknown today. (Courtesy of Texas State Library and Archives Commission 1979/181-07)

MAP KEY

1 *c.*0500hrs: Santa Anna orders the attack to begin and four columns of Mexican infantry stand up and advance across about 300yd of open ground to the Alamo.

2 *c.*0505hrs: Recoiling from the ferocity of Texian artillery and small-arms fire, Mexican infantrymen in all four columns fall back in confusion. Travis is shot dead defending the north wall.

3 *c.*0510hrs: Observing his infantry being thrown back, Santa Anna orders his reserves forward to reinforce the attack on the north wall.

4 *c.*0515hrs: Encouraged by reinforcements, the Mexican infantry under Cos, Castrillon, and Romero renew their attack and scale the walls.

5 *c.*0520hrs: The Texians fall back from the north and west walls to the barracks buildings, jail cell, armory and hospital building, and chapel.

6 *c.*0525hrs: Texian artillerymen attempt to turn the 18-pounder cannon in the redoubt in the southwest corner inward toward the Mexicans in the parade ground, but are bayoneted to death by elements of the Matamoros, Jiménez, and San Luis Potosí battalions who have scaled the wall.

7 *c.*0525hrs: Morales's troops also break through the palisade, killing Harrison's Tennesseans, including David Crockett.

8 *c.*0530hrs: Some Texians attempt to break out of the Alamo and advance into the prairie to the east where they are killed by elements of the Dolores Regular Cavalry Regiment.

9 *c.*0535hrs: Mexican infantrymen fire several captured cannon at the buildings occupied by the remaining defenders and blow the doors down. Firing a volley with their muskets, they charge into the buildings with fixed bayonets and kill the occupants.

10 *c.*0540hrs: Sick in the small hospital room in the officers' quarters east of the main gate, James Bowie is bayoneted to death as Mexican infantrymen enter that building.

11 *c.*0545hrs: Using the captured Texian 18-pounder cannon, the Mexicans destroy the wall in front of the chapel, following which their infantry charge into the chapel after firing a volley of musketry. Turning their cannon 180 degrees, the artillerymen commanded by Dickinson fire into the Mexicans before being overrun and killed.

12 *c.*0605–0620hrs: Mexican infantrymen bayonet or shoot those Texians still alive. Santa Anna arrives in the fort and orders his buglers to sound the *alto el fuego* ("cease fire"), but the slaughter continues for a further 15 minutes.

Battlefield environment

The land west and north of the Alamo sloped gently down toward the San Antonio River. The quarter of San Antonio known as La Villita lay to its south, and some of the northernmost *jacales* (huts) of that community faced the west wall of the Alamo. The soil in the area was a fine sandy loam with a darker clay mixture in the *acequia* (irrigation ditch) to its north, west, and south. The ditch was mostly dried up at this time. There were cultivated fields to the southeast of the fort.

Founded in 1718, the Mission of San Antonio de Valero at the Alamo was founded to convert the local American Indians to Christianity, and eventually became a community of Spanish, Mexican, and American Indian Catholics. Following secularization at the end of the 18th century, and during the Mexican struggle for independence from Spain the buildings fell into disuse and the church remained unfinished, but were fortified by both the Mexicans and Texians during the Texas Revolution. (LC-DIG-highsm-27796)

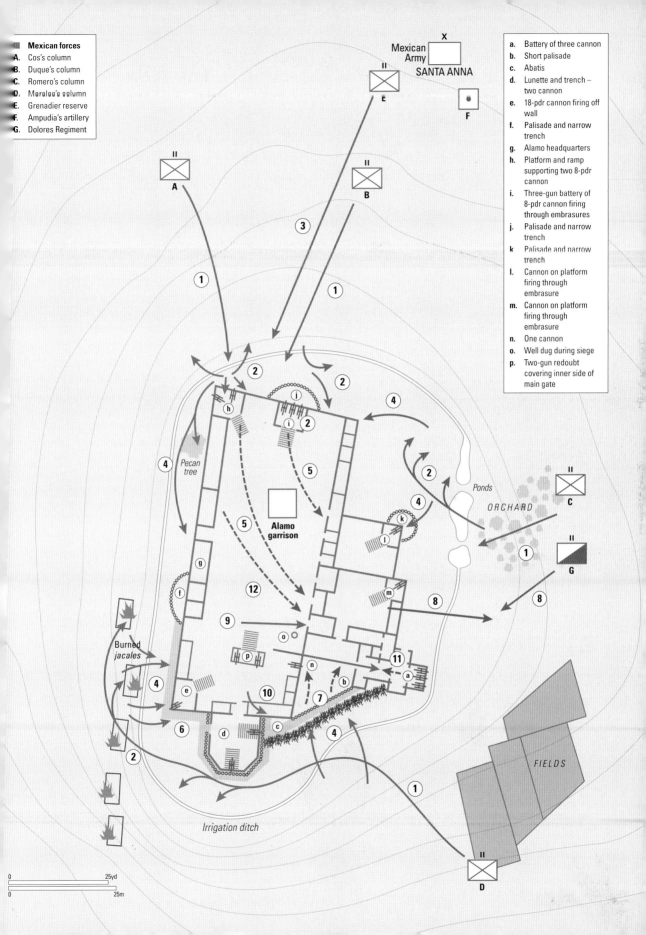

Mexican forces
- **A.** Cos's column
- **B.** Duque's column
- **C.** Romero's column
- **D.** Morales's column
- **E.** Grenadier reserve
- **F.** Ampudia's artillery
- **G.** Dolores Regiment

Mexican Army
SANTA ANNA

a. Battery of three cannon
b. Short palisade
c. Abatis
d. Lunette and trench – two cannon
e. 18-pdr cannon firing off wall
f. Palisade and narrow trench
g. Alamo headquarters
h. Platform and ramp supporting two 8-pdr cannon
i. Three-gun battery of 8-pdr cannon firing through embrasures
j. Palisade and narrow trench
k. Palisade and narrow trench
l. Cannon on platform firing through embrasure
m. Cannon on platform firing through embrasure
n. One cannon
o. Well dug during siege
p. Two-gun redoubt covering inner side of main gate

Pecan tree

Alamo garrison

Ponds

ORCHARD

Burned jacales

FIELDS

Irrigation ditch

0   25yd
0   25m

INTO COMBAT

As the first light of dawn appeared in the eastern sky at about 0500hrs, Santa Anna signaled to Bugler José María González, of the Sappers Battalion, and the *¡Adelante!* ("Forward!") call rang out, which was echoed immediately by all the other buglers in the army. At the same time, the officers waved their swords and yelled *¡Arriba!* ("Attack!"), and the four assault columns stood up and moved toward their designated point of attack. According to 1st Lieutenant José Enrique de la Peña, serving as an aide to Duque who commanded the second column: "The columns advanced with as much speed as possible; shortly after beginning the march they were ordered to open fire while they were still out of range, but there were some officers who wisely disregarded the signal" (de la Peña narrative 1836: n.p.).

Inside the fort, officer-of-the-day Captain John J. Baugh had just started inspecting the lines when he heard the bugle calls and cries, and raised the alarm. As the Mexicans crossed the open ground yelling *¡Viva Santa Anna!* and *¡Viva La Republica!* the Texians posted as sentries opened fire, while their comrades were swiftly awakened and poured out to man the cannon and defense works. Of these frantic moments in the half-light of dawn, 2d Sergeant Manuel Loranca, of the Matamoros Regular Infantry Battalion, recalled: "In the act of assault a confusion occurred, occasioned by darkness, in which the Mexican troops fired on each other" (*EDR*, July 24, 1898: 6:2).

The assault was so sudden that the Texians only had time to discharge four of their 18 cannon in the walled defenses. One of the 8-pounders fired from the northwest corner of the fort swept away most of a company of the Aldama Regular Infantry Battalion. Within the ranks of the column under Morales that attacked the south wall and main gate, Private Felix Nuñez recalled:

Found in the notebooks of artist Henry A. McArdle, this albumen print of Susannah Dickinson, survivor of the Alamo, was produced in Austin, Texas, by photographer Hamilton B. Hillyer. According to Dickinson: "The enemy three times applied their scaling ladders to the wall, twice they were beaten back. But numbers and discipline prevailed over valor and desperation. On the third attempt they succeeded, and then they came over 'like sheep'" (*AG*, May 14, 1836: 2:2). (Courtesy of Texas State Library and Archives Commission 1979/181-07)

The division of the army on the west side was the first to open fire. They fired from the bed of the river [irrigation ditch] … The first fire from the cannon of the Alamo passed over our heads and did no harm; but as the troops were advancing the second one opened a lane in our lines at least fifty feet broad. Our troops rallied and returned a terrible fire … (*SADE*, June 30, 1889: 3:3)

As the second column advanced toward the north wall, de la Peña observed that "a single cannon volley did away with half the company of chasseurs [voltigeurs] from Toluca … Captain José María Herrera, who commanded it, died a few moments later and Vences, its lieutenant, was also wounded" (de la Peña narrative 1836: n.p.). Another volley left many gaps among the ranks at the head of the column, one of them being Duque. Wounded in the thigh and nearly trampled

to death by his own men, he was replaced in command by General of Brigade Manuel Fernandez Castrillon.

Furthermore, the Mexican assault columns found that their poorly made ladders were too flimsy to bear the weight of several men at once, and rather than use them, those at the north end of the fort began massing in the dead ground at the foot of the wall. Thus, as the Texians discharged their previously loaded firearms, they were forced to lean over to shoot which in turn exposed them to Mexican fire. Included among the Texian casualties at this stage was Travis. With his armed servant Joe by his side, he fired down into the seething mass below, only to be shot in the head. According to Joe, Travis fell dead and slid down the embankment of soil that had been thrown up to strengthen the wall.

Approaching from the east, the column commanded by Romero was exposed to severe fire from the cannon firing through a hole in the wall of the cattle pen, and most of the Mexicans fell back into the orchard while others joined the closely packed troops against the north wall. At the same time, the men in the column led by Cos came under equally severe fire and also fell back or joined those massing at the foot of the north wall.

Advancing on the southern end of the fort, some of the fourth column under Morales approached the low palisade with an *abatis* of felled trees in front and came under heavy fire from the Tennessee Mounted Volunteers, led by Captain William B. Harrison. Among those attacking the lunette in front of the main gate, 1st Sergeant Becerra observed: "The doors of the Alamo

From *Our Pioneers and their Daring Deeds*, published in 1887, this engraving entitled "The Defence of the Alamo" depicts Texians standing their ground as Mexican troops scramble over their fortifications. (Internet Archive)

Martin Perfecto de Cos

Born in Veracruz on October 1, 1800, the son of an attorney, Martin Perfecto de Cos became an Army cadet at the age of 20, and rose through the ranks to general of brigade in 1833. In September 1835, he was ordered by his brother-in-law Santa Anna to investigate the refusal of settlers at Anahuac, Texas, to pay customs duties, which is regarded as a prelude to the Texas Revolution. Dispersing the legislature of Coahuila and Texas, Cos landed 300 men at Matagorda Bay and established his headquarters in San Antonio de Béxar, where he declared his intention to end Anglo-American resistance in Texas. Following a failed attempt to arrest several Texian critics of Santa Anna, his small Mexican army was besieged for about two months by Texian forces under Stephen F. Austin and Edward Burleson, and surrendered on December 11, 1835. Released after pledging not to oppose further the Constitution of 1824, which had recently been repealed by Santa Anna, Cos and his troops were ordered to march out of Texas.

On his return to Mexico City, Cos was treated as a hero. Breaking the terms of this agreement, he commanded a column in the attack on the Alamo on March 6, 1836, and on April 21, reinforced Santa Anna at San Jacinto with about 500 troops. Taken prisoner in the general surrender, he was later released and returned to Mexico. During the Mexican–American War (1846–48) he commanded a small Mexican garrison at Tuxpan, which he failed to defend against a US landing party under Commodore Matthew C. Perry on April 18, 1847. He died in Minatitlán, Veracruz, on October 1, 1854, while serving as commandant general of the Tehuantepec, Mexico.

building were barricaded by bags of sand as high as the neck of a man, the windows also. On the top of the roofs of different apartments were rows of sand bags to cover the besieged" (quoted in Hanford 1878: 29). Of the moment he reached the wall at the southwest corner of the fort, Becerra recalled that he and his comrades "planted scaling-ladders, and commenced ascending; some mounted on the shoulders of others; a terrific fire belched from the interior; men fell from the scaling-ladders by the score, many pierced through the head by balls, others fell by clubbed guns. The dead and the wounded covered the ground" (quoted in Hanford 1878: 30). Mauled by the artillery and small-arms fire from the Alamo defenders, much of the fourth column sought shelter behind the burnt-out *jacales* near the southwest corner of the fort.

Seeing the bulk of his infantry reeling back in confusion, Santa Anna feared they might be routed and ordered his reserves forward to the piercing notes of the *Deguello*, the haunting bugle call signifying "no quarter." After being kept at bay for about 15 minutes, the reinforced Mexican infantrymen began to scale the walls. Those under Cos made an oblique move to the right and attacked several points along the west side of the fort. Among those who first made it over the west wall was General of Brigade Juan Valentin Amador, second-in-command of the column led by Cos, and artillery commander Lieutenant Colonel Pedro Ampudia, who encouraged more men to follow them. Inspired by the bravery of these officers, more Mexicans scaled the wall and scrambled through gun ports. Meanwhile, elements of Romero's troops climbed the wall at the northeast corner of the fort and also captured the cannon in the corner of the cattle pen.

Also by this time, elements of the Matamoros, Jiménez, and San Luis Potosí battalions under Morales had fought their way over the palisade wall on the southeast corner of the fort. After discharging their muskets, Harrison's Tennesseans fell back, furiously wielding their firearms as clubs and brandishing knives as they became surrounded by Mexican bayonets. At

David Crockett

Born on August 17, 1786, and of mostly French-Huguenot ancestry, David Crockett grew up in East Tennessee, working as a cattle drover, farmhand, and teamster from the age of 12. In 1813 he enlisted as a private for three months' service in the Creek War (1813–14) with the 2d Regt. Mounted Gunmen, West Tennessee Volunteers, and participated in the battle at Tallushatchee (1813) under Major General Andrew Jackson where 186 Red Stick Creeks, including women and children, were killed. During the next five years, he gained a reputation as a hunter and frontiersman, and saw further military service as a soldier and scout under Jackson in Georgia and Florida, rising to the rank of lieutenant colonel in the Tennessee militia. His election to the Tennessee State Legislature in 1821 was a steppingstone to three nonconsecutive terms in the US House of Representatives during 1827–35. His exploits made him a national figure and the subject of numerous books, songs, and a play.

Concerned about the exaggerations of his life, Crockett wrote an autobiography entitled *Narrative of the Life of David Crockett, of the State of Tennessee*. Published in 1834, the title page contained the following advice by the author: "I leave this rule for others when I'm dead, Be always sure you're right – THEN GO AHEAD!"

During this period in politics Crockett vehemently opposed many of the policies enacted during the presidency of Andrew Jackson, especially the Indian Removal Act of 1830, which authorized the movement of southern Native American nations to federal territory west of the Mississippi River in exchange for the white settlement of their ancestral lands. Opposition to this policy led to Crockett's defeat in the 1831 elections. Although re-elected in 1833, he narrowly lost again in 1835, which prompted his angry departure to Texas, there to participate in the Texas Revolution and meet his death at the Alamo on March 6, 1836.

this point, it is surmised that David Crockett, among others, fell mortally wounded. When his mutilated remains were found lying halfway between the chapel and the two-story armory/hospital building at the end of the battle, he was surrounded by at least 16 dead Mexican infantrymen.

The flanking movements of the Mexicans forced the Texians to fall back from the north and west walls and into the barrack buildings, jail cell, armory, hospital, and chapel, where they manned specially made loopholes in the thick stone walls. Meanwhile, Texian artillerymen at the southern end of the fort attempted to turn the 18-pounder in the redoubt in the southwest corner inward toward the Mexicans swarming in the parade ground. These Texians were overrun and bayoneted to death within minutes by infantrymen under Morales, who had by this time also scaled the southwest walls. Of this stage in the action Becerra recalled:

> Our troops, inspired by success, continued the attack with energy and boldness. The Texians fought like devils. It was at short range – muzzle to muzzle – hand to hand – musket and rifle – bayonet and "Bowie knife" – all were mingled in confusion. Here a squad of Mexicans, there a Texian or two. The crash of firearms, the shouts of defiance, the cries of the dying and the wounded, made a din almost infernal. (Quoted in Hanford 1878: 29)

According to Nuñez: "By this time the court yard, the doors, the windows, roof and all around the doomed Alamo became one rocking mass of armed humanity. Each one of us vied with the other for the honor of entering the Alamo first" (*SADE*, June 30, 1889: 3:3). Some Texians attempted to break out of the fort and advance into the prairie to the east. In his report to Santa Anna, Sesma stated that they were slaughtered by the Dolores Regular Cavalry Regiment. Of this incident, Loranca recalled:

Sixty-two Texans who sallied from the east side of the fort were received by the lancers and all killed. Only one of these made resistance; a very active man armed with a double-barrel gun and a single-barrel pistol, with which he killed a corporal of the lancers named Eugenio. These were all killed by the lance, except one, who ensconced himself under a bush, and it was necessary to shoot him. (*EDR*, July 24, 1898: 6:2)

For the next half-hour, the Mexicans fought to gain control of the rest of the Alamo. According to Becerra: "The Texians defended desperately every inch of the fort – overpowered by numbers, they would be forced to abandon a room; they would rally in the next, and defend it until further resistance became impossible" (quoted in Hanford 1878: 29).

During their hasty withdrawal the Texians had no time to spike their cannon, and Amador and Ampudia ordered several of them loaded and trained on the buildings harboring the remaining defenders. With troops manning one of these guns, Becerra recalled: "A detachment of which I had command had captured a piece of artillery. It was placed near the door of the hospital, doubly charged with grape and canister, and fired twice" (quoted in Hanford 1878: 30). Blowing the door off, the Mexicans fired a volley with their muskets, and then charged in with fixed bayonets. Becerra continued: "There was a long room on the ground-floor – it was darkened. Here the fight was bloody. It proved to be the hospital. The sick and wounded fired from their beds and pallets … We entered and found the corpses of fifteen Texians.

Ten women remained within the ranks of the garrison of the Alamo during the battle on March 6, 1836. "Battle of the Alamo" by Percy Moran, published in 1912, depicts one of them alongside the defenders. (LOC LC-USZC4-2133)

On the outside we afterwards found forty-two dead Mexicans" (quoted in Hanford 1878: 30). Chief Surgeon Amos Pollard, of the Permanent Texan Volunteers, probably died attempting to defend those in his care at this point.

Having been quarantined in a smaller hospital room in the officers' quarters east of the main gate, Bowie was too sick and weak to offer any resistance. As the Mexicans entered that building, he was bayoneted to death and his body was dragged out into the Plaza (*NHG*, April 19, 1836: 1:3).

The last Texians to die were probably 11 men manning the battery of three cannon in the chapel. A shot from the captured 18-pounder fired by the Mexicans destroyed the wall in front of the building. The Mexican infantry then fired a volley with their muskets and charged into the chapel. Still manning their cannon which had been turned around to face the enemy, Texian artillery commander Almeron Dickinson's men were overrun and bayoneted to death.

According to Susannah Dickinson, one of 15 civilians to survive the battle, the wounded Ordnance Officer, Major Robert Evans, attempted to prevent the gunpowder magazines from falling into Mexican hands, but was killed and his torch extinguished only inches from the gunpowder. Had he succeeded, the blast would have destroyed the chapel and killed the women and children hiding in the sacristy. As the Mexicans entered the chapel, one of the young sons of artilleryman Anthony Wolf stood to pull a blanket over his shoulders, but was mistaken for an adult and shot dead. Also seeking refuge was Private Brigido Guerrero, of Seguín's cavalry company, who had deserted from the Mexican Army in December 1835. Locking himself in a cell, he was spared after convincing the soldiers he had been held prisoner by the Texians.

In his journal of events, de la Peña recorded that "the scene of extermination" went on for an hour before "the curtain of death covered and ended it" shortly after 0600hrs (de la Peña narrative, 1836, n.p.). Even

Entitled "At the Alamo's Brave Battle," this romanticized depiction by Robert J. Onderdonk of the last desperate moments of the Texian defense at the Alamo, and featuring David Crockett using his musket "Old Betsy" as a club, was published in 1910 in *Combats and Conquests of Immortal Heroes*, by Charles M. Barnes. (LOC F394.52 B3)

then some Mexican infantrymen continued to shoot, killing several of their comrades in the confusion. The Mexican commanders were unable to stop the bloodlust and appealed to Santa Anna for help. Although the general made an appearance in the Alamo, the violence continued and the buglers were finally ordered to sound the "retreat." For a further 15 minutes after that, Mexican soldiers inspected each fallen Texian and bayoneted or shot anyone who moved. According to an exaggerated account by Loranca:

> There in front of the fosse [or road leading into San Antonio] were gathered the bodies of all those killed in the fort, making a total of 283 persons … and here they were ordered to be burned, there being no room in the … burying-ground, it being all taken up with the bodies of upwards of 400 Mexicans who were killed in the assault. (*EDR*, July 24, 1898: 6:2)

An early estimate of the Mexican dead and wounded was provided by Dr. Bernard, who was captured at Coleto Creek on March 20, 1836, and, with Dr. Jack Shackelford, commander of the Red Rovers, was asked by the Mexican Colonel Domingo de Ugartechea, commander at Goliad, to help tend the Mexican wounded at the Alamo. Arriving there under escort on April 19, 1836, Bernard recorded in his journal, what

> a pretty piece of work "Travis and his faithful" have made of them. There are now about one hundred here of the wounded. The surgeon tells us that there were five hundred brought into the hospital the morning they stormed the Alamo, but I should think from appearances there must have been more. I see many around the town who were crippled, – apparently two or three hundred, – and the citizens tell me that three or four hundred have died of their wounds. We have two colonels and a major and eight captains under our charge who were wounded in the assault. (Quoted in Wooton 1898: 630)

An official account of the Mexican dead and wounded is found in the first edition of Filisola's *Memoirs*, published in 1848–49, which stated that there were more than "70 dead men and three hundred wounded" (Filisola 1848–49: 389). The most accurate estimate of Mexican casualties comes from a list produced by Andrade and included in the second edition of Filisola's *Memoirs*, which stated that 60 were killed and 251 wounded (Filisola 1849: 10).

Mexican accounts exaggerated the total number of Texians killed at the Alamo. Colonel Juan Nepomuceno Almonte, one of Santa Anna's *aides-de-camp*, wrote in June 1836: "On the part of the enemy the result was, 250 killed, and 17 pieces of artillery – a flag; muskets and fire-arms taken" (*TH*, June 27, 1836: n.p.). Based on a detailed analysis of rosters of military units making up the Alamo garrison, plus lists of identified individuals within its walls, 203 Texian soldiers and civilians were killed, one soldier was captured, and 15 civilians survived.

OPPOSITE
This detail from the McArdle painting "Dawn at the Alamo" shows David Crockett wielding his clubbed musket, while sheltering under the rampart at right, Susannah Dickinson, wife of Texian artillery commander Almeron Dickinson, clutches her 15-month-old baby Angelina. Next to her in a red shirt is Ben, the servant of Lieutenant Colonel William B. Travis. (Carol M. Highsmith Archive, LC-DIG-highsm-27909)

This wood engraving published in *"Go Ahead!" Davy Crockett's Almanack, 1837*, is believed to be the earliest known illustration of his death at the Alamo. (National Portrait Gallery, Smithsonian Institution: NPG.85.139.14)

Coleto Creek

March 19–20, 1836

BACKGROUND TO BATTLE

After the fall of the Alamo, Santa Anna devised a three-pronged strategy designed to overwhelm what remained of the Texian forces. General of Brigade Urrea would continue his march along the south coast with 1,400 men; Brevet General of Brigade Gaona would advance across the northern part of Texas with 700 men; and Santa Anna and General of Brigade Sesma would lead 1,200 men through the center of Texas.

When news of the Alamo reached Major General Houston at Gonzales, he immediately ordered a retreat westward. Meanwhile, the position of the Texian garrison in Fort Defiance, or Presidio La Bahía, at Goliad under Colonel Fannin was rendered untenable following Urrea's victories at San Patricio and Agua Dulce. Having not yet received orders to retreat, however, Fannin continued to fortify Fort Defiance.

On March 10, 1836, Fannin received a message from some settlers at Refugio, about 30 miles south of Goliad, requesting help to evacuate the area. In response, Fannin sent Captain Amon B. King with 28 men of the Georgia Battalion. Upon arrival, King's company was attacked by ranchers and herdsmen led by Carlos de la Garza operating as advance cavalry for Urrea. Seeking cover in the ruined church of the Mission of Nuestra Señora del Refugio, King sent a messenger back to Goliad requesting reinforcements. With the arrival of the messenger at Fort Defiance during the early hours of March 12, Fannin sent Lieutenant Colonel William Ward and the remaining four companies of the Georgia Battalion to relieve King. On the same day, Fannin received orders from Houston to abandon and destroy Fort Defiance and withdraw 27 miles east to Victoria. Determined to await the return of King and Ward, Fannin sent word to them either to fall back to Goliad, or to

make their way to Victoria across the Guadalupe River. He was also reinforced by Captain Albert C. Horton and a company of 30 mounted rangers from Matagorda.

Despite sending out several scouting parties, Fannin had received no word from King and Ward by March 16. As a last resort, Frazer volunteered to ride south on "a good horse … to ascertain the state of affairs, and pledged himself, if alive, to return in twenty-four hours with intelligence" (Wooton 1898: 618). The next day, Dr. Bernard wrote in his diary:

> At length, about four P.M., Captain Frazier [*sic*], true to his word, arrived, and gave us full and explicit information … Colonel [*sic*] Ward had reached Refugio and relieved Captain King. Instead of immediately turning back, they unfortunately delayed their return, and Captain King started off with his company to destroy some ranches where the people had showed hostility. Colonel Ward was soon after attacked by a body of Mexican troops and driven into the church from which he had but a short time before released Captain King. He now found that Urrea with his division was about him and endeavoring to dislodge him … Ward and his gallant men defended themselves, and repulsed all attacks made upon them. When night came, finding their ammunition exhausted, they succeeded in eluding the vigilance of the Mexicans, silently left the church and retreated upon the coast. Captain King, on reaching the ranche [*sic*] he intended to destroy, met with opposition and rather got worsted in the fight. He made a circuit to get back to Refugio, reached it in the night and found it occupied by the Mexicans. They then crossed the river and endeavored to retreat from the place, but got lost on the prairie, and, after wandering all night, found themselves in the morning at a place call 'Malone's Ranch.' They had been watched and followed by a party of spies, and soon a force was around them that made resistance useless. They surrendered and were immediately started for Goliad. They had proceeded but a few hundred yards when a halt was made in the prairie; King and his comrades were taken out and shot. Such were the results of the expedition. (Quoted in Wooton 1898: 618–19)

Entitled "View of the Goliad Presidio before Bahia del Espiritu Santo," this pencil drawing by Lino Sanchez was produced in 1834 and is one of the earliest representations of Goliad, the site of of Presidio La Bahía, or Fort Defiance, before the Texas Revolution. Eager to fight the Mexicans, the garrison amounted to about 720 men, consisting of the Georgia and Lafayette volunteer battalions, each composed of five companies, a militia company from Refugio commanded by Captain Hugh M. Frazer, a company of Texian regular infantry led by Captain Ira J. Westover, and a detachment of Texian regular artillery under captains Stephen Hurst, Benjamin H. Holland, and Joseph Schrusnecki. (Jean Louis Berlandier Papers. Yale Collection of Western Americana, Beinecke Rare Book and Manuscript Library)

In response, Fannin immediately ordered a retreat to Victoria to begin the next morning. Shortly afterward, scouts arrived back and reported that a large Mexican force was in the vicinity. As evacuation preparations continued throughout the night, patrols were sent out to watch for imminent attack. At daybreak on March 18, a detachment of Mexican cavalry was seen reconnoitering the vicinity of the fort and Horton was ordered out with a party of mounted rangers to drive them off. Of this action, Dr. Bernard recorded:

> I went with several others to the top of the church, which commanded a fine view of the country for several miles around. Colonel [sic] Horton now giving chase to his late pursuers, followed them over to the north side and on over the prairie; occasionally a shot was fired, until the parties were lost from our view in the distance. After a while they made their appearance coming back, but now the condition was again changed. The Mexicans were following our men and pressing them very hard; but they succeeded in reaching the old *Aranama* (a mission), and getting under the shelter of its walls, made a stand ... The Mexicans, numbering about one hundred, drew up in front at a safe distance and opened a fire, which was returned. Captain [Jack] Shackleford [sic] now started out with his company to relieve Colonel Horton, and our artillerymen got one of their guns mounted on the wall and brought to bear on the Mexican party. A shot was fired at them, which fell short, but they thought it wise to draw off. They soon disappeared, and we saw no more of them. (Quoted in Wooton 1898: 619–20)

The Texian preoccupation with enemy cavalry on March 18 delayed the retreat to Victoria, and Dr. Bernard concluded that "the horses were jaded and tired down, and our oxen, that had been gotten up to draw the cannon and baggage-carts, were left all day without food" (quoted in Wooton 1898: 620).

At 0630hrs on March 19, Fannin began his retreat from Goliad amid heavy fog. Of preparations for his departure, Private Zachariah M. Brooks, of the Red Rovers, recalled that "the fort was set on fire, and its wooden defences destroyed; but the wall was left entire ..." (*NDI*, June 10, 1836: 1:5) The nine pieces of brass artillery Fannin took with him were described by artillery officer Captain Holland as consisting of "one six inch howitzer, three short sixes, two long and two short fours, with several small pieces for throwing musket balls" (*HR*, June 14, 1836: 1:1). This was confirmed by Brooks, who referred to "several field pieces, sixes, fours, and swivels" (*NDI*, June 10, 1836: 1:5). These were either dragged by oxen or carried in carts, along with 1,000 muskets. Unfortunately, Fannin neglected to ensure that a sufficient supply of food and water was transported, and the guns and baggage carts were pulled by tired and undernourished animals.

It took about 2½ hours for the Texians to get their whole column across the Lower Ford of the San Antonio River about a mile east of the fort. The whole operation was held up when one of the cannon sank into the mud and had to be dragged manually to the opposite bank. With many of their wagons and carts overloaded, the Texians were forced to abandon much of what they set out with.

By about 0900hrs, Fannin's column was able to resume its march. Progressing about 4 miles, it reached and forded Manahuilla Creek. According to Dr. Bernard, it pushed on for another mile until it reached "a patch of green grass where there had been a late burn," where, at about 1200hrs, Fannin ordered that the oxen be allowed to graze for about an hour (quoted in Wooton 1898: 620). Recalling this part of the march, Private Abel Morgan of Westover's regulars, in charge of the hospital wagon, stated: "We had to haul our cannon with oxen and they were wild and contrary and by the time we had gone three or four miles we had to stop and rest them" (*NCA*, May 15, 1849: 1:2). At this point Fannin faced objections from Duval and Westover, who believed they should have continued until the column reached the cover of woodland at Coleto Creek.

This portrait of Colonel James W. Fannin, Jr., commander of the Texian army at Coleto Creek, is believed to have been completed while he was a cadet at the US Military Academy at West Point, New York, during the 1820s. (Dallas Historical Society M.63.3.1)

Meanwhile, due to the thick fog Urrea did not realize the Texians had evacuated the fort until about 1100hrs. In order to catch up with them, he left his artillery and some infantrymen in Goliad, beginning his pursuit with 80 cavalry and 360 infantry. His mounted scouts soon located the retreating Texians grazing their oxen east of Manahuilla Creek, and reported their numbers as smaller than expected. Wrongly believing that Fannin had not evacuated his entire garrison at Goliad, Urrea sent 100 infantrymen back to help secure Presidio La Bahía, while ordering up his artillery for the impending action.

During the march Fannin had deployed Horton's mounted rangers to guard the head, flanks, and rear of his column. Not sufficiently alert, the four men in the rear were unaware that the Mexican cavalry was closing on them. Resuming the march after resting the oxen, Fannin's column progressed about another 2 miles until it reached a low ridge, where another cart broke down and its cargo had to be transferred. By this time the timberland at Coleto Creek was in sight, and an advance guard including most of Horton's mounted rangers was sent to reconnoiter it.

Meanwhile, Horton's small rearguard had dismounted and fallen asleep, and were nearly trampled under the hooves of the approaching Mexican cavalry. Making their escape, all but one of Horton's men galloped past the column and deserted their comrades. According to Dr. Bernard, only "one of them (a man named [Herman] Ehrenburg [*sic*], a German), joined us" (quoted in Wooton 1898: 620).

At 1330hrs, the Mexicans came into view of Fannin's column. Urrea recorded in his diary:

> I overtook the enemy and succeeded in cutting off their retreat with our cavalry, just as they were going to enter a heavy woods from where it would have been difficult, if not impossible, to dislodge them … My troops, though fatigued by the rapidity of the march, were filled with enthusiasm at seeing the enemy … Although our force was inferior and we had no artillery, the determination of our troops made up the disparity. Expecting the artillery and our munitions to reach us soon, agreeable to instructions given, I decided to engage the enemy at once. (Quoted in Castañeda 1928: 223)

1 *c.*1400hrs, March 19: Urrea's Mexican army catches up with and surrounds Fannin's column as it retreats from Fort Defiance at Goliad.

2 *c.*1410hrs, March 19: Fannin orders his column to form a defensive position 300yd north of the road where his wagons and carts are drawn up into a hollow square with the Mobile Greys facing north, the Red Rovers and San Antonio Greys facing west, the Mustangs and Refugio Militia Company facing east, and Westover's Regulars facing south. Artillery pieces are placed at each of the four corners of the square, and Fannin and staff establish their headquarters behind the wagons at its center.

3 *c.*1410hrs, March 19: The hospital wagon is abandoned outside the hollow square with sick men aboard. Several men would successfully defend it during the battle.

4 *c.*1420hrs, March 19: Although his artillery has not caught up with his advance, Urrea decides to attack. As a feint, he orders part of the Jiménez Regular Battalion, commanded by Lieutenant Colonel Mariano Salas, to advance slowly on the western face of the Texian square formation, while other elements of the battalion, commanded by Colonel Juan Morales, march in column formation around to the north of the Texian square, and the San Luis Potosí Active Militia Battalion plus grenadiers of the Jiménez Regular Battalion, led by Urrea, march in column formation to its south. Meanwhile, the Mexican cavalry, under Colonel Gabriel Núñez, trot in column formation to a position northeast of the Texians.

5 *c.*1430hrs, March 19: With all three infantry battalions in position, Urrea issues the command via bugle call to change front from column to line of battle, fix bayonets, and charge.

All three infantry battalions charge at the Texian square, but falter and withdraw when met by fierce musketry fire.

6 *c.*1445hrs, March 19: Seeing the Texians entrenching their position, Urrea orders Núñez's cavalry to charge at the northwest corner of the Texian square. Although some of the Mexican cavalry reach the Texian lines, they are repulsed by artillery fire and withdraw.

7 *c.*1830hrs, March 19: After the failure of several more Mexican attacks during the next hour, and with his troops running low on gunpowder, Urrea orders one more simultaneous attack before dark on all four faces of the Texian square using cavalry and infantry, which again fails.

8 *c.*1930hrs, March 19: With nightfall descending, Urrea issues orders for all his troops to retire and encamp in the woodland to the east, leaving both cavalry and infantry pickets at strategic points surrounding the Texians. He orders bugle calls to be sounded throughout the night to deprive the Texians of sleep.

9 *c.*0400hrs, March 20: The Mexican artillery, consisting of three 12-pounder guns, arrives and is placed with infantry support behind a rise in the ground southeast of the Texian square.

10 *c.*0700hrs, March 20: At dawn the Mexican artillery opens fire and sends chain-shot over the heads of the Texians.

11 *c.*0710hrs, March 20: The wounded Fannin realizes his troops cannot withstand cannon fire and surrenders to Urrea and staff having received a guarantee his troops would be treated as prisoners-of-war, and sent to the nearest port to be transported to the United States within eight days of being marched back to Goliad.

Battlefield environment

The ground on which Fannin was forced to make a stand consisted of a low-lying area of prairie about a half-mile across with the absence of any other natural cover and concealment other than tall grass. A screen of oak-tree woodlands stood about a quarter-mile to his east and northwest. The Mexicans under Urrea controlled the surrounding countryside, including access to the crucial water supply of Coleto Creek. A slight ridge to the southeast offered cover for Mexican infantry, plus artillery after its arrival.

Entitled "The Mexicans attempted two more charges," this illustration by Victor S. Pérard was originally published in 1902 in *With Crockett and Bowie; or, Fighting for the Lone-Star Flag: A Tale of Texas*. Mexican lancers attack the hollow square formed by infantry commanded by Fannin during the battle of Coleto Creek on March 19, 1836. Mexican infantry are shown advancing in the distance. (Author's collection)

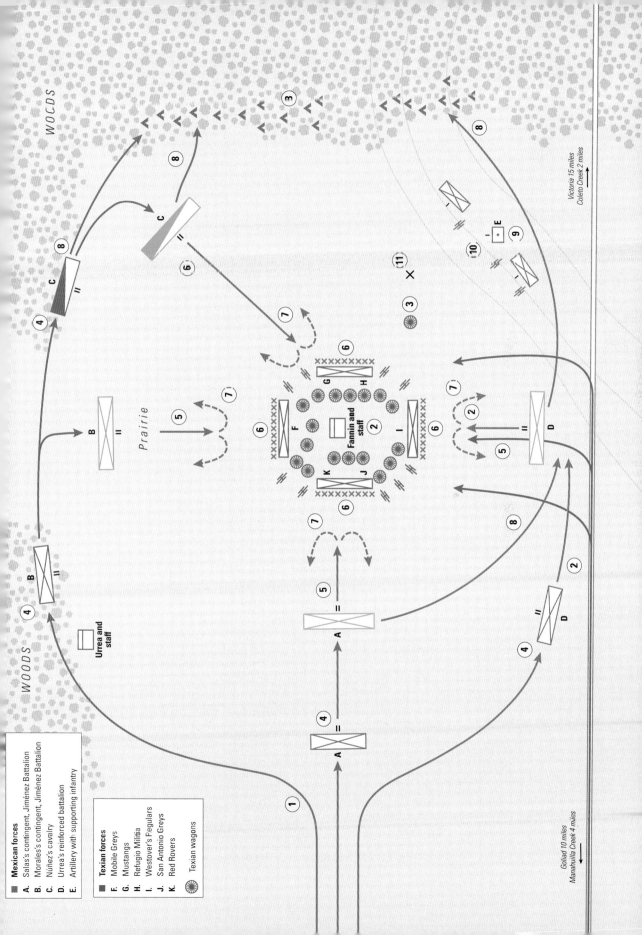

Mexican forces

A. Salas's contingent, Jiménez Battalion
B. Morales's contingent, Jiménez Battalion
C. Núñez's cavalry
D. Urrea's reinforced battalion
E. Artillery with supporting infantry

Texian forces

F. Mobile Greys
G. Mustangs
H. Refugio Militia
I. Westover's Regulars
J. San Antonio Greys
K. Red Rovers

Texian wagons

WOODS

Prairie

Urrea and staff

Fannin and staff

WOODS

Victoria 15 miles
Coleto Creek 2 miles

Goliad 10 miles
Manahuilla Creek 4 miles

INTO COMBAT

Instead of continuing his march to the woodland at Coleto Creek, where his infantry might have fended off the Mexican cavalry, Fannin halted the column again and ordered one of his cannon into action with the enemy still three-quarters of a mile away. Dr. Bernard recalled that "a six-pounder was unlimbered, from which three shots were fired … but, as we perceived, fell short" (quoted in Wooton 1898: 620). From his viewpoint with the hospital wagon at the head of the column, Morgan observed: "We halted and fired several rounds with one of the cannons … and went on perhaps a mile further" (*NCA*, May 15, 1849: 1:2).

A running battle ensued during which the Mexicans caught up with the Texian column. Captain Holland recalled that "almost simultaneously they were descried upon both flanks, evidently with the design of surrounding us. The enemy had now formed a semi-circle on our right and left, and as we had no means of moving our artillery but by stubborn and worn-out oxen, were fast surrounding us" (*HR*, June 14, 1836: 1:1–2). As Horton and the few mounted rangers galloped off in hopes of returning with reinforcements from Victoria, Fannin ordered all his artillery to the rear of the column to keep up a retreating fire, under cover of which he attempted to make farther progress with the Mexicans at his flanks and rear, and closing around his front (*LV,* June 13, 1836: 2:5). Cut off from his advance guard with a force reduced to about 382 rank and file, and opposed by 500 Mexican cavalry and 200 infantry, Fannin had little choice but to order a halt and make a stand (*NDI*, June 10, 1836: 1:5).

Fannin ordered the column to move 300yd north of the road on to the prairie in a low valley about a quarter-mile across, where their wagons and carts were drawn up in an irregular circle with the infantry forming the perimeter of a rough hollow square, with staff and headquarters at their center, and with artillery placed at each of its four corners. The Mobile Greys faced north, the Red Rovers and San Antonio Greys faced west, the Mustangs and Refugio Militia Company east, while those facing south were Westover's Regulars. Each side of the square was composed of three ranks with each man in the front rank armed with a musket with fixed bayonet to repel a Mexican cavalry charge. Those in the other ranks were armed with a mixture of weapons, including hunting rifles, carbines, and pistols.

During this maneuver, Morgan's wagon, filled with four sick or injured men and their gear, was the lead vehicle. He recalled: "There was immediately a square formed, and as they took the oxen from the cannon, instead of securing them they were turned loose and got away … I had two yoke oxen and was the foremost team. So when they halted and formed a square, I was left forty or fifty yards from the square to the East" (*NCA*, May 15, 1849: 1:2). Within seconds both Morgan's oxen were shot down by Mexican musketry fire and his Mexican driver deserted to the enemy. Having passed his musket to an officer as the rest of the column moved off the road, Morgan was forced to abandon his sick comrades and hastened into the square. He would return to defend the hospital wagon and the men therein with four other men during the ensuing battle.

To distract the enemy while he launched attacks from the north and south, Urrea ordered part of the Jiménez Regular Battalion, led by Lieutenant

Colonel Mariano Salas, to advance in column formation on the western face of the Texian square. Meanwhile, the bulk of the Jiménez Regular Battalion, under Colonel Juan Morales, would attack from the north. At the same time, the grenadiers of the Jiménez Regular Battalion and the San Luis Potosí Active Militia Battalion, under Urrea, would attack from the south. The Mexican cavalry, commanded by Colonel Gabriel Núñez, would charge from the north and east.

Waiting for the attack within the ranks of the Mustangs, Private John C. Duval observed:

> When the Mexicans had approached … our lines they formed into three columns, one remaining stationary, the other two moving to our right and left, but still keeping at about the same distance from us … When the two moving columns … were opposite to each other, they suddenly changed front and … with trumpets braying and pennons flying, charged upon us simultaneously from three directions. (Duval 1892: 41)

Owing to the ferocity of the Texians' musketry fire, all three columns of Mexican infantry faltered and made only slow progress toward the Texian lines. Some Mexicans got within bayonet-reach of Fannin's formation, but all were eventually driven back, and the flag of the Jiménez Regular Battalion was captured after its bearer fell.

Meanwhile, the Texians began to entrench their position and threw up breastworks using dead animals and knapsacks that they covered in soil. Observing this, Urrea ordered a cavalry charge on the north and east sides of the square. As the Mexican cavalry deployed to the east, Duval recalled that "a long dark line was seen to detach itself from the timber behind us, and another at the same time from the timber to our left. Some one near me exclaimed, 'Here come the Mexicans!' and in … a little while, we perceived that these dark lines were men on horseback, moving rapidly towards us" (Duval 1892: 40).

Facing north within the ranks of the Mobile Greys, Ehrenberg saw the Mexican cavalry break into a canter. He wrote later they

> gave us a volley from their carbines, to which … we paid no attention as the balls flew in respectable distance over our heads. Only occasionally one would whiz up entirely exhausted as if it were breathing its last breath and strike the ground in front of us without even knocking up any dust. Only one … whistled through between me and the next man … and tore off a part of the cap of my friend, Thomas Camp, who, after me, was the youngest man in the army. We remained completely passive and let the enemy approach who fired volley after volley at us [;] as he came nearer our artillery officers … patiently waited for the

Worn by a soldier of the Dolores Regular Cavalry Regiment, this black hardened patent-leather helmet with tricolor pompon in brass holder has a black goat-hair plume in brass comb at the left, brass "eagle and snake" plate at the front, and brass chin scales fixed by a rayed "lion's head" disc at each side. The Dolores Regular Cavalry Regiment took part in the storming of the Alamo under Colonel Ventura Marar, and smaller elements of the unit fought at Coleto Creek and San Jacinto. (Phil Collins Texana Collection, courtesy of The Texas General Land Office C-2020-0268)

"Here come the Mexicans!"

Mexican view: Having observed the Texians entrenching their square formation by piling dead animals and knapsacks at their front and covering them with soil, General of Brigade José de Urrea has joined Colonel Gabriel Núñez and leads a cavalry charge from the northeast involving 250 officers and men. After firing wildly with their carbines as they approach the waiting Texians at a canter, some of the Mexican horsemen falter while others break into a gallop and reach the Texian lines, where they are met with cannon and fierce musket and rifle fire. Enveloped with powder smoke, they reel and fall back in confusion.

Texian view: In the ranks of the Mustangs along the east-facing side of the Texian square, Private John C. Duval hears a comrade nearby exclaim "Here come the Mexicans!" The Texians receive a largely ineffectual fire from carbines as the Mexican cavalry approach at a canter. Duval then observes multiple flashes of steel as the Mexicans draw sabers or level lances and break into a charge. Of the final moments of the action, he recalled that the Mexican horsemen were unchecked until their foremost ranks reached the Texian lines, but impact at close quarters from the Texian cannon, musket, and rifle fire was so rapid and destructive that many Mexicans fell leaving the ground covered in places with horses and dead men (Duval 1892: 40–41).

time when they could reply to the unholy greetings to advantage. (Ehrenberg 1845: 119)

With the artillery, Captain Holland recollected: "We were ordered not to fire until the word of command was given, in order to draw the enemy within rifle shot. We reserved our fire for about 10 minutes, and several were wounded in our ranks previous to our firing" (*LV*, June 13, 1836: 2:5). Ehrenberg recalled: "The moment arrived, our ranks opened, and the artillery hurled death and destruction among the enemy. Their horses, to which the confusion of battle was a terror, reared up wildly" (Ehrenberg 1845: 119). Holland continued: "The wind was blowing slightly from the N.E. and the smoke of our cannon covered the enemy, under which they made a desperate charge, but were repulsed with a very severe loss" (*LV*, June 13, 1836: 2:5).

Of the final moments of the cavalry charge, Duval with the Mustangs recalled that the Mexicans were unchecked until their foremost ranks were in "actual contact in some places with the bayonets of our men. But the fire at

The gala or dress tailcoat of General of Brigade Juan Morales, who commanded troops at the Alamo and Coleto Creek with the rank of colonel, is based on that decreed for Mexican general officers on October 16, 1823. It was made of dark-blue wool with scarlet facings edged with gold embroidery of intertwined laurels, palms, and olives on the collar, plastron front, and cuffs. This is repeated on the dark-blue flaps on the pockets at the top of the tails. (San Jacinto Museum courtesy of Mr. and Mrs. George A. Hill, Jr.)

close quarters from our muskets and rifles was so rapid and destructive, that before long they fell back in confusion, leaving the ground covered in places with horses and dead men" (Duval 1892: 41). In his diary, Urrea wrote:

> I found the enemy prepared to meet us … with scorching fire from their cannons and rifles. Our horses were in very poor condition and ill-suited for the purpose, but the circumstances were urgent and extraordinary measures were necessary. My efforts, however, were all in vain, for after repeated trying to make the dragoons effect an opening in the enemy ranks, I was forced to retire. (Quoted in Castañeda 1928: 225)

Urrea subsequently placed his cavalry in "a position where it could continuously threaten the enemy, avoiding, as far as possible, their fire" (quoted in Castañeda 1928: 225).

According to Dr. Bernard, who was tending the Texian wounded, the action continued without a break from 1500hrs until dark (roughly 1930hrs), during which time the Mexican infantry and cavalry made further charges, the latter "forming behind on a little rise of ground about four or five hundred yards off and then galloping up at full speed" (quoted in Wooton 1898: 621). With his infantry running out of ammunition, Urrea decided to order a simultaneous charge on all fronts, later recording:

> I gave the necessary orders and as the bugler gave the signal agreed upon, all our forces advanced with firm step and in the best order. I placed myself again at the head of the cavalry … All our troops advanced to within fifty and even forty paces from the square. So brave an effort on the part of our courageous soldiers deserved to have been crowned with victory; but fortune refused to favor us. The enemy redoubled its resistance with new vigor … I ordered all our infantry to fix bayonets and to maintain a slow fire with whatever powder remained. For almost an hour, this unequal contest was kept up, then I finally gave the order to retire. (Quoted in Castañeda 1928: 226)

Captain Holland recalled:

> Thus was the battle kept up; and upon the repulse of each charge, column upon column of the enemy were seen to fall like bees before smoke. Here would be seen horses flying in every direction without riders; and there, dismounted cavalry making their escape on foot, while the field was literally covered with dead bodies. It was a sorry sight to see our small circle – it had become muddy with blood. Col. Fannin had been so badly wounded at the first or second fire as to disable him. The wounded were shrieking for water, which we had not to give them. The fight continued until dusk, when the enemy retreated, leaving us masters of the field … (*LV*, June 13, 1836: 2:5)

On March 19, Fannin suffered seven dead and 371 prisoners of war, which included about 55 wounded. The Mexicans sustained about 50 killed and about 140 wounded.

As night closed in, Urrea placed his infantry behind a gentle slope about 300yd from the Texians. He detailed cavalry and infantry pickets to points

Serving as garrison troops in the northern border states of Mexico from Texas to California, the Presidial Permanent Cavalry companies were part of the mounted force riding into battle at Coleto Creek on March 19, 1836. Their dress uniform consisted of a short blue tailcoat with red collar and cuffs, gray or dark-blue trousers with wide red seam stripes, and black felt hat with white worsted band (Courtesy Anne S.K. Brown Military Collection, Brown University)

where they might observe enemy movement, and ordered his musicians to sound *Sentinel Alerto* ("false bugle calls") to keep the Texians awake and on edge during the hours of darkness (Castañeda 1928: 226). Meanwhile, the Texians spent the night strengthening the trenches and breastworks on all four sides of their square. Although wounded in the abdomen, Fannin proposed cutting his way through the enemy lines at daybreak and resuming the march; but it was soon discovered that so many horses had been killed or wounded, and that the oxen had strayed away, it was impossible to transport the wounded.

At sunrise, as the Mexicans prepared to renew their attack, some chain-shot whistled over the heads of the Texians, heralding the arrival of the Mexican artillery. Almost immediately, both sides waved white flags. Urrea and the wounded Fannin, accompanied by aides, met "at a proper distance from their respective armies" and, according to Dr. Field, the Mexican general "embraced Col. Fanning [*sic*], and said, 'Yesterday we fought; but to-day we are friends'" (*CC*, August 20, 1836: 1:1).

San Jacinto

April 20–21, 1836

BACKGROUND TO BATTLE

Learning of the surrender of Colonel Fannin on March 20, 1836, the Texian Government fled north from Gonzales to Harrisburg on Buffalo Bayou. Thousands of Texian settlers followed suit in what became known as the "Runaway Scrape." Realizing his army was the last hope for an independent Texas, and to avoid being outflanked by Urrea, Major General Houston retreated 120 miles northeast across the Navidad and Colorado rivers, finally arriving by March 28 at the Brazos River, opposite Groce's Plantation, with a force that eventually increased to 900 men. For this action he faced much criticism from Texas Interim President David G. Burnet, who sent Secretary of War Thomas J. Rusk to urge him to fight, stating: "The enemy are laughing you to scorn. You must fight them; you must retreat no further. The country expects you to fight; the salvation of the country depends on your doing so" (*TS*, April 5, 1840: 1:3).

Meanwhile, Santa Anna remained in San Antonio de Béxar. After receiving news that acting President Miguel Barragán had died on March 1, 1836, he considered returning to Mexico City to reaffirm his position, but concern that Urrea might be seen as a rival for the presidency following his victories convinced Santa Anna to remain in Texas to oversee the final phase of the campaign personally. Leaving only a small garrison to hold San Antonio de Béxar, he left on March 29 to join General of Brigade Sesma in the march to San Felipe de Austin, on the Brazos River. By April 7, their combined force of about 700 men reached that place, where they captured a Texian soldier who informed Santa Anna that the Texians planned to retreat farther east if the Mexican army crossed the Brazos.

Unable to cross the Brazos because three companies of Texians were dug in on the opposite bank of the river at Groce's Plantation, Santa Anna left Sesma's troops to guard that point and made a difficult crossing of the Brazos at Fort Bend, about 25 miles farther south, following which he marched 35 miles toward Harrisburg in hopes of capturing the interim Texas government. Arriving with a small cavalry escort at the temporary Texian capital at about 2300hrs on April 15, Santa Anna found the town virtually deserted, and was informed that Burnet and his cabinet had fled only a few hours earlier in the direction of New Washington, on the Galveston Bay coast. While Harrisburg was put to the torch, Mexican cavalry continued the pursuit and arrived just in time to see Burnet and his party shove off in a rowboat making for Galveston Island. Although the Texians were in carbine range, the Mexican officer ordered his men not to open fire as there were women in the boat.

By this time, with the Texian government forced off the mainland and with no means of communicating with its army, Santa Anna believed the rebellion was in its final death throes. To strengthen his army further, he dispatched orders to General of Division Filisola, at Fort Bend, to send up General of Brigade Cos with about 500 infantrymen. When Santa Anna's cavalry scouts reported that Houston's army had left Groce's Plantation and was heading for the Trinity River via Lynch's Ferry, on the San Jacinto River, from where it might board a ship and join Burnet on Galveston Island, he decided to block the Texian army's path by seizing Lynch's Ferry.

In the meantime, the Texian army continued its march eastward and on April 18 arrived at a burning Harrisburg. That same day, Texian cavalry scouts Captain Henry W. Karnes and Private Erastus "Deaf" Smith captured two Mexican couriers carrying dispatches revealing that Santa Anna was only a few miles away, having marched with only one division from New Washington in the direction of Lynch's Ferry. Drawing his men up into a hollow square, Houston delivered a rousing speech to prepare his men for battle, exhorting them to "Remember the Alamo!" and "Remember Goliad!"

ABOVE LEFT
The Matamoros Regular Infantry Battalion flag was flown at the Alamo, Coleto Creek, and San Jacinto. Embroidered with "Batallon Matamoros Permanente," it was named in 1835 for Father Mariano Matamoros, a military commander during the Mexican War of Independence against Spain (1821). Both these flags were captured during the battle of San Jacinto on April 21, 1836. (Courtesy of Texas State Library and Archives Commission. Texas State Archives, Acc. No. 306-4032)

ABOVE RIGHT
The reverse of the tricolor flag carried by elements of the Guerrero Regular Infantry Battalion at San Jacinto on April 21, 1836. The flag bears the Mexican coat of arms below the inscription "Pe.[ermanente] Batallon Guerrero." In 1835 this unit was named for the Mexican revolutionary hero Vicente Guerrero, and was a veteran unit by 1836. (Courtesy of Texas State Library and Archives Commission. Texas State Archives, Acc. No. 306-4033

MAP KEY

1 *c.*0900hrs, April 20: The Texian army reaches Lynch's Ferry, and then withdraws a half-mile and sets up camp in woodland along the south bank of Buffalo Bayou.

2 *c.*1200–1400hrs, April 20: The Mexican army arrives and its advance guard encounters Texian pickets, who open fire and withdraw into the woods. Santa Anna orders elements of the Toluca Militia Battalion to deploy as skirmishers while the remainder of his infantry and his artillery are deployed in the prairie and woodland facing the Texians, and his cavalry cover the left flank. Santa Anna's artillery exchanges fire with Texian artillery, and his infantry is repulsed as it advances in column.

3 *c.*1600hrs, April 20: The Mexican army withdraws about a half-mile and establishes camp on the open prairie.

4 *c.*1930hrs, April 20: Shortly before sunset, Texian cavalry led by Colonel Sidney Sherman mounts an unsuccessful raid on the Mexican encampment. Texian skirmishers advance out of the woods to cover the cavalry withdrawal, thereby revealing to Santa Anna the strength of Houston's force.

5 *c.*0000–0900hrs, April 21: During the night, Santa Anna extends his right flank, placing three infantry companies on the bank of the San Jacinto River. The Matamoros Regular Battalion takes position at the center behind a breastwork. His artillery is placed behind a breastwork; his cavalry, plus select infantry companies, protect his left flank.

6 *c.*0900hrs, April 21: Cos arrives, reinforcing the Mexican army with 400 troops. Much of this force rests and sleeps after an overnight march.

7 *c.*1200hrs, April 21: Texian volunteers destroy Vince's Bridge, cutting off Mexican means of withdrawal.

8 *c.*1530hrs, April 21: Houston orders his infantry to march in column formation northeast under cover of woodland until opposite the Mexican right flank. Serving as a distraction, the Texian cavalry is drawn up in view facing the Mexican left flank. Still covered by the ridge line, the Texian infantry march out on to the prairie and wheel right to form in line of battle.

9 *c.*1600hrs, April 21: With much of the Mexican army resting, a bugler sounds the "Alarm" as the whole Texian battle line advances over the ridge and into view.

10 *c.*1600hrs, April 21: The Texian artillery advances until within 175yd of the Mexican position and fires grapeshot.

11 *c.*1600hrs, April 21: The Texian cavalry charges at the Mexican left wing and routs the Mexican cavalry.

12 *c.*1605hrs, April 21: The Texian infantry reach the Mexican lines and hand-to-hand fighting ensues.

13 *c.*1625hrs, April 21: The lines of the Mexican infantry break and retreat in panic.

14 *c.*1630–1730hrs, April 21: The Texians pursue the routed Mexican infantry for about an hour, driving them into the marshland and waters of the San Jacinto and McCormick's Lake.

15 *c.*1800hrs, April 21: Over 700 Mexican soldiers are allowed to surrender to the Texian army, although Santa Anna escapes and is captured the next day.

Battlefield environment

The location chosen by Houston to do battle with Santa Anna consisted of tall prairie grassland and marshland at the confluence of the San Jacinto River and Buffalo Bayou, both of which were flooded at the time. The area along Buffalo Bayou had many thick oak groves separated by marshes. This type of terrain was familiar to the Texians, but quite alien to the Mexican soldiers. The prairie in front of Houston's woodland encampment was interrupted by a ridgeline that obscured the Mexican view of the whole battlefield.

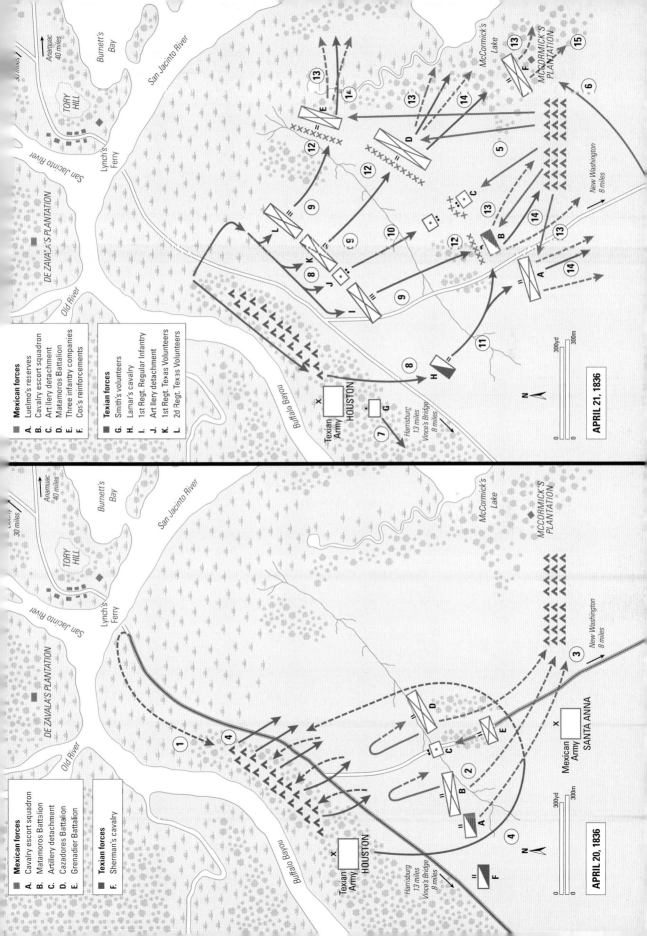

This military uniform coat belonged to Colonel Sidney Sherman, commander of the 2d Regt. Texas Volunteers at the battle of San Jacinto. Not part of any known regulations for the Texian Army, it is made from lightweight blue wool lined with white silk. It has a black velvet collar, shoulder straps, and cuffs, all edged with gold-twist trim. There are two rows of five brass General Staff buttons on each side, each with an engraved federal eagle surrounded by stars. (San Jacinto Museum and Battlefield Association)

INTO COMBAT

The Texian army rested until the early hours of April 19 on the north bank of the flooded Buffalo Bayou. In his after-battle report, Houston stated: "The main body effected a crossing over Buffalo Bayou, below Harrisburg, on the morning of the 19th, having left the baggage, the sick, and a sufficient camp guard in the rear. We continued the march throughout the night making but one halt in the prairie for a short time without refreshment" (*DA*, June 16, 1836: 2:4). Continuing their march at daylight on April 20, the Texians reached Lynch's Ferry and then withdrew a half-mile to woodland along the south bank of Buffalo Bayou, where they established "Camp Safety." Scouts reported the approach of the Mexican army at about noon.

As the Mexican army advanced toward Lynch's Ferry, Santa Anna ordered his infantry to remove their knapsacks and leave them by the roadside. At about 1300hrs his advance guard encountered Texian pickets, who opened fire and withdrew into the woods. Unable to ascertain enemy numbers, Santa Anna ordered the Toluca Militia Battalion to deploy as skirmishers, and opened fire with his cannon. Houston later reported that Santa Anna

> took a position with his infantry and artillery in the centre, occupying an island of timber; his cavalry covering the left flank. The artillery then opened on our encampment, consisting of one double fortified medium brass twelve pounder. The infantry in column advanced with the design of charging our lines, but were repulsed by a discharge of grape and canister from our artillery, consisting of two six pounders. (*DA*, June 16, 1836: 2:4).

During the exchange of artillery fire, both Lieutenant Colonel James C. Neill, commanding the Texian guns, and Captain Fernando Urriza, commanding the Mexican gun, were seriously wounded. After further small-arms fire on the Texian left flank, the Mexican army withdrew about three-quarters of a mile and began to construct breastworks and establish an encampment in an exposed position near the bank of the San Jacinto River.

In his after-battle report, Santa Anna wrote: "I wished to draw him into a field of battle suited to my purpose, and in consequence withdrew about one thousand yards distance, to an eminence affording a favorable position, with abundance of water, on my rear, a thick wood on my right, and a large plain on my left" (quoted in Delgado 1921: 24). Critical of his commanding general's leadership, Delgado later commented that the "camping ground of His Excellency's selection was, in all respects, against military rules. Any youngster would have done better" (Delgado 1921: 9).

Shortly before sunset, Colonel Sidney Sherman led about 85 Texian cavalry, including Secretary of War Rusk, out to reconnoiter the Mexican position and attempt to capture their cannon. After receiving a volley from the left of the enemy's infantry, they clashed with their cavalry. During the ensuing melee, Rusk dismounted to reload his rifle and had to be saved from capture by Texian cavalry commander Colonel Mirabeau B. Lamar (who later became the second President of the Republic of Texas). Lamar also rescued another Texian, who had been thrown from his horse. Having had two men wounded, one mortally (Private Owlyn J. Trask) and another seriously

(Private Devereaux J. Woodlief), the Texian cavalry withdrew back into the woodland.

At the same time, numerous Texian infantrymen disobeyed orders and advanced out of the woods to cover the withdrawal of their cavalry, which angered Houston as by doing so they gave the enemy a better estimate of their strength and location. The Texians were equally annoyed that their commander had not committed them to a full battle. In response, Santa Anna deployed two companies of voltigeurs as skirmishers. As night descended around 1930hrs, the Texian infantry also retreated back into the woodland, with one man wounded (Thomas Utly, Co. F, 1st Regt. Texas Volunteers).

During the night, Santa Anna deployed his troops to best advantage. He extended his right flank by placing three infantry companies in the woods skirting the marshes on the bank of the San Jacinto. The Matamoros Regular Battalion formed his main line of battle at the center behind a breastwork constructed of earth and grass mixed with wooden pack saddles, knapsacks, and sacks of corn. He secured his left flank by positioning his cannon behind a breastwork about 5ft high, constructed of packs and baggage. The cavalry was also drawn up on his left wing to protect the artillery. A reserve of select companies under Lieutenant Colonel Santiago Luelmo was also formed behind his left wing.

A private in the Texian Army, scout and pioneer Private Erastus "Deaf" Smith fought throughout the Texas Revolution, and performed valuable service during the battle of San Jacinto by supervising the destruction of Vince's Bridge over Vince Bayou, which cut off the main route of retreat west for the Mexican army after its defeat on April 21, 1836. He earned his nickname due to hearing loss in childhood. Portrait by Thomas J. Wright. (San Jacinto Museum and Battlefield Association)

At 0900hrs on April 21, Cos arrived with 400 infantry reinforcements composed of regulars from the Aldama and Guerrero battalions and militia from the Guadalajara and Toluca battalions. Although many of these were raw recruits with little or no battle experience, they increased the total strength of Santa Anna's army to about 1,500 men as opposed to a Texian force of 908. According to Delgado, their arrival was greeted with "the roll of drums and with joyful shouts" (Delgado 1921: 10). As the morning passed with no sign of a Texian attack, Santa Anna permitted his reinforcements to stack arms, remove accouterments, and rest in the woods behind the Mexican right flank. The remainder of Santa Anna's command were also lulled into a false sense of security, causing Delgado to comment: "His Excellency and Staff were asleep; the greater number of the men were, also, sleeping; of the rest, some were eating, others were scattered in the woods in search of boughs to prepare shelter. Our line was composed of musket stacks. Our cavalry were riding bare-back, to and from water" (Delgado 1921: 10).

Meanwhile, Houston ordered Smith and a small group of volunteers to destroy Vince's Bridge, a wooden structure over Vince Bayou, about 8 miles west near Harrisburg, thus cutting off the Mexican withdrawal and escape route back to the Brazos River.

At 1530hrs, Houston ordered his infantry to assemble, and marched them in column formation northeast under cover of woodland. Once opposite the Mexican right flank and still behind the ridge line that rendered them invisible to the enemy, they were marched out toward the Mexican position and formed in line of battle. The 1st Regt. Texas Volunteers, commanded by Colonel Edward Burleson, was assigned to the center. The 2d Regt. Texas Volunteers, led by Sherman, formed the left wing. The artillery, under Colonel George W. Hockley, was wheeled into place on Burleson's right. The 1st Regt. Regular Infantry, under Lieutenant Colonel Henry W. Millard, formed the right wing. Meanwhile, Lamar's cavalry was ordered to distract the enemy by assembling in view of their right flank. Private George B. Erath, Co. C, 1st Regt. Texas Volunteers, recalled:

> Being ever ready, our lines were formed at once, but in the low ground out of sight of the Mexicans. Perhaps a delay of half an hour occurred till the position was perfect as to rank and number … Orders to wheel in detached companies and march in double file by heads of companies followed, descending into a sink of ground then reaching a small eminence two or three hundred yards from the Mexicans, we were ordered to wheel by left in front … which brought us to the top of the hill. (*Memoirs* 1886: n.p.)

As the Texians came into view of the Mexicans, Delgado recalled:

> At this fatal moment, the bugler on our right signaled the advance of the enemy upon that wing … I stepped upon some ammunition boxes, the better to observe the movements of the enemy. I saw that their formation was a mere line in one rank, and very extended. In their center was the Texas flag … Their cavalry was opposite our front, overlapping our left. (Delgado 1921: 10)

In his after-battle report, Santa Anna wrote: "I was in a deep sleep when I was awakened by the firing and noise; I immediately perceived we were attacked, and had fallen into frightful disorder" (quoted in Delgado 1921: 25).

According to Hockley, who replaced the wounded artillery commander Neill, the Texian artillerists "marched up within 175 yards, [un]limbered our pieces and gave them the grape and canister, while our brave riflemen poured in their deadly fire" (*NB & NW*, May 20, 1836, 2:5). As they opened fire, the "Twin Sisters" hit the Mexican artillery breastwork exploding an ammunition box. Within the artillery ranks as an enlisted man was future Confederate General Benjamin McCulloch. Meanwhile, Lamar's horsemen charged and routed the cavalry on the Mexican right wing.

Serving with the 1st Regt. Texas Volunteers, Erath recalled: "As the Mexicans shot high, nearly all the harm … to us was done during the descent of the hill to the Mexican lines" (*Memoirs* 1886: n.p.). Private James M. Hill of Co. H of the same regiment recollected: "We all knew the battle cry … and it was shouted with a will" (Hill Papers n.p.). Fighting with Co. F, Private Alfred Kelso recalled: "We were marched in forty yards of their breastworks before we were allowed to fire …" (Kelso 1836: 18).

Clad in buckskin and waving his saber, Houston was riding ahead of his infantry when his horse was shot from under him. While being helped on to another mount, a Mexican musket ball hit his left ankle. Ignoring the wound and with his boot filling with blood, he continued to ride into battle urging his men on.

At the Texian center, Private William C. Swearingen, Co. B, 1st Regt. Regular Infantry, recalled:

> The infantry was ordered to trail arms, and advance until within 50 yds of the enemy before we fired … when within about 20 steps of the enemy's line we were ordered to charge … & brought our guns to the proper position[.] the enemy gave way except about 60 men round the canon & protected by breast work of corn sacks, salt, barells [*sic*] of meal & boxes of canister shot. They fell by the bayonet & sword in one mangled heap … it was nothing but a slaughter. (Swearingen Letters, April 23, 1836)

Remarking on the impact of the Texian attack, Private George Fennell, of the Velasco Blues, Captain William S. Fisher's Company, 1st Regt. Texas Volunteers, observed: "so sudden was our charge on their lines that they instantly gave way …" (*Fennell Letter*, November 14, 1836).

At the head of part of the Guerrero Battalion, Colonel Juan Almonte attempted unsuccessfully to organize resistance within the ranks of the panicked Mexican army, but surrendered to Texian Secretary of War Rusk who rode into battle with the 2d Regt. Texas Volunteers Cavalry Corps.

Of the closing stages of fighting, Erath continued:

> We reserved our fire. The whole Mexican line was in full flight by the time I got a second shot. Our men advanced rather in disorder and drove the Mexicans across a boggy slew where many fell … Our men had ceased firing because we were too closely mixed with the Mexicans. At a point of timber across the slew, which was by this time bridged with bogged horses on which we crossed, a Mexican officer of high rank, flourished his sword, made a grand appeal to rally his men, but was shot down, and the men who turned to face us again resumed their flight, only to be overtaken and shot. I do not like to dwell on these scenes. (*Memoirs* 1886: n.p.)

Produced in 1901 by Henry A. McArdle, this painting of the battle of San Jacinto was discovered in an attic in 2009, and depicts the fierce clash of arms on April 21, 1836, as the Texian army commanded by Major General Houston reaches the Mexican line, taking them almost completely by surprise. Houston waves his hat as he urges his troops on to victory while the Texian flag of the Newport Volunteers, also known as the Buck Eye Rangers, is held aloft above the whole scene. Mounted on a brown steed, Private Erastus "Deaf" Smith plunges his sword into Lieutenant Colonel Esteban Mora as he attempts to rally the Mexican infantry. Brandishing his sword above his head is Captain Andrew Briscoe, commanding Co. A, 1st Regt. Regular Infantry. (The Picture Art Collection/ Alamy Stock Photo)

"Remember the Alamo!"

Viewed through the eyes of a Mexican mounted officer, the long thin line of the 2d Regt. Texas Volunteers commanded by Colonel Sidney Sherman shout "Remember the Alamo!" as they approach the Mexican battle line at the double-quick, firing at point-blank range. Some Texians break through the breastwork, constructed from wooden pack saddles, knapsacks, and sacks of corn, and engage in a desperate hand-to-hand struggle with remnants of the Toluca Militia Battalion, who reel back in disarray.

A dismounted Mexican general of brigade attempts to rally his men, ordering them to fix bayonets and stand their ground or open fire. A Mexican standard-bearer is captured as he attempts to wave the flag of the Toluca Militia Battalion. Other Mexican troops cast away their weapons and retreat in panic, treading on those who have thrown themselves to the ground in an attempt to avoid the grapeshot and musket balls flying around them. As *aide-de-camp* Brevet Colonel Pedro Delgado recalled of the chaos in the Mexican ranks: "I endeavored to force some of them to fight, but all efforts were in vain – the evil was beyond remedy; they were a bewildered and panic-stricken herd" (Delgado 1921: 10).

While the slaughter was going on at the center of the Mexican army, the right and left wings were routed by the Texians with equal success. According to Swearingen, many of the Mexicans in the woods to the right attempted to swim the San Jacinto, but were "surrounded by our men, and they shot every one … as soon as he took [to] the water, and them that remained they killed as fast as they could load & shoot them, until they surrendered" (Swearingen Letters, April 23, 1836).

Seeing that further resistance was fruitless, the Mexican cavalry at left spurred their horses and dashed toward Vince's Bridge, but were horrified to find it had been destroyed. Some of the horsemen spurred their mounts down the steep bank, while others dismounted and plunged into the stream. As they came up behind the Mexicans, the Texian cavalry poured a deadly fire into the struggling mass of men and horses.

According to Houston's after-battle report, the action lasted about 18 minutes from the time his infantry clashed with the Mexicans until they were in complete control of their lines and encampment (*DA*, June 16, 1836: 2:4). After riding back to "Camp Safety," Houston is reported to have fainted from loss of blood from his ankle wound; he was helped off his mount by Hockley and treated by his surgeons.

The Texians sustained only seven killed and 37 wounded. The Mexican dead amounted to about 650, which included one general, four colonels, three lieutenant colonels, five captains, and 12 lieutenants. About 700 escaped the battlefield, including Santa Anna, Cos, and four of Santa Anna's aides. Some 300 of these men were captured before nightfall, and the rest were rounded up during the next two days (Hardin 1994: 215). The Mexican wounded amounted to 208 and included six colonels, three lieutenant colonels, seven captains, and one cadet. Weapons, equipage, and animals captured amounted to 900 Tower muskets, 300 sabers, 200 pistols, 300 mules, and 100 horses, plus $1,200 in silver (Dixon *et al.* 1932: 11). The next day, Santa Anna was captured hiding in a marsh wearing civilian clothing and making his way toward Vince's Bridge. Brought before the wounded Houston, he bowed and declared, "I am General Antonio López de Santa Anna, a prisoner of war, at your disposal" (Baker 1873: 61).

Analysis

THE ALAMO

The battle at the Alamo stands without doubt as a memorial to the courage and patriotic sacrifice of its defenders in the Texas Revolution. A garrison of approximately only 201 officers and men, plus *c*.18 civilians, faced a much larger force of 2,117 Mexican regular and militia soldiers, and fought until the last defender was killed. Nevertheless, San Antonio de Béxar held little significance for the defense of other Texian settlements farther north. Even if Travis and his brave garrison had held the fortified mission, Santa Anna might easily have left a token force to pin them down while he marched the main body of his troops in pursuit of Houston and the rest of the Texian forces.

Furthermore, the delay resulting from Santa Anna's insistence on taking the Alamo did not slow Houston's advance appreciably. Although the Mexicans

Entitled "Dawn at the Alamo," this detailed painting by Henry A. McArdle was commissioned by Moses A. Bryan, nephew of Stephen F. Austin (*DDS*, January 24, 1875: 2:5), and is an inaccurate reconstruction looking south of the chaos and slaughter following the entrance of Mexican troops into the Alamo fortifications at about 0520hrs on March 6, 1836. According to the artist's notes, Travis is shown on the rampart at right in "a death grapple with a Mexican standard-bearer, a struggle in which both are going down along with the banner which its bearer had vainly attempted to plant." A Mexican waving the "Blood Red Flag," a symbol of no quarter, is shot down on the exaggeratedly raised gun platform at center. (Carol M. Highsmith Archive, LC-DIG-highsm-27909)

spent two weeks besieging and attacking the Alamo, Houston made slow progress in recruiting and training the Texian army at Gonzales, which was hardly more ready for battle in early March than it had been in late February 1836. The Texians would certainly have benefited had their ranks included the men who instead died at the Alamo.

The defenders of the Alamo might have fought their way out had they chosen to do so, especially during the early days of the siege, although their chances of fighting off Santa Anna's cavalry on the plains beyond the fort were minimal. Owing to a lack of vigilance, the Mexicans allowed couriers carrying desperate requests for help to slip through their lines during the hours of darkness on at least 12 occasions and permitted several groups of reinforcements to enter the fort. Despite this, by the end of February the Alamo was mostly surrounded and its defenders were trapped.

Certainly, Santa Anna's losses were considerably greater than those of the Texians, but his army was much larger and could afford such heavy casualties. The fall of the Alamo achieved precisely what the "Napoleon of the West" intended. As news spread throughout settlements, it struck terror into the hearts of thousands of Anglos and *Tejanos* in south and central Texas and caused the "Runaway Scrape" as they fled toward Louisiana.

COLETO CREEK

Events leading to the battle at Coleto Creek could have been avoided had Fannin evacuated Fort Defiance at Goliad sooner than March 19, 1836. Unfortunately, his attempt to rescue Texians at Refugio – and insistence on waiting for news from, or the return of, the Georgia Battalion – added to his delay in acting. This exposed him to criticism for ignoring the order to withdraw issued by Houston on March 12, and ultimately led to his military defeat at Coleto Creek (Wooton 1898: 618).

When Fannin finally abandoned Fort Defiance, he committed several major errors. Although he burned the fort's wooden ramparts, he failed to destroy its stone defenses, which left a viable military installation for the Mexicans to reoccupy. Having neglected to feed and water the oxen readied to pull the guns and wagons during the skirmish on March 18, Fannin also overloaded many of his wagons, and failed to ensure that a sufficient supply of food and water was carried by his column when it set out. This led to both men and animals suffering greatly, requiring the column to halt several times to allow the animals to graze during the hours leading to the action at Coleto Creek. Thus, Urrea's troops were more easily able to catch up with the lumbering Texian column.

Some Texians, including Fannin, wrongly believed the Mexicans were an inferior foe, and that they would not pursue them. Even after the Texian column was overtaken and forced to make a stand, Holland felt confident the Texians had "a great advantage over the Mexicans, they having no artillery" (*LV*, June 13, 1836: 2:5), which had got lost but finally caught up with the cavalry and infantry on March 20.

Without artillery support on the first day of the battle, problems increased for the Mexicans by virtue of an order for some of their infantrymen to carry fewer than four rounds in their cartridge boxes to lighten their load. Despite this, their courage in attack at Coleto Creek made up for their lack of ammunition (Castañeda 1928: 223). With the arrival of three Mexican 12-pounder guns from Goliad on March 20, and with all his animals killed, the wounded Fannin had no choice but to surrender.

The articles of capitulation guaranteed the Texians would be treated as prisoners of war, and sent to the nearest port to be transported to the United States in eight days after being marched back to Goliad. Instead of honoring these terms, Santa Anna ordered all prisoners, except for surgeons who tended the Mexican wounded and those who assisted them, to be shot as traitors according to Mexican law, and one week later, on March 27, 1836, an estimated 342 Texians were executed, including Fannin. Known as the Goliad Massacre, this action horrified world opinion. As a result, this brought *de facto* recognition to the Republic of Texas by the leading European powers.

SAN JACINTO

Enraged by events at the Alamo and the atrocity committed at Goliad, the Texian army facing Santa Anna on April 21, 1836, was motivated by a powerful desire for revenge. Aware that there were still about 4,000 Mexican troops in Texas, Houston wisely concealed the size of his army by posting it in woodland along the bank of the San Jacinto River. Meanwhile, Santa Anna committed a cardinal sin. Anxious to capture the Texian government, which had joined the flight east, he divided his army, leaving troops under Sesma at the Brazos River, and allowing Houston to corner him at the confluence of the San Jacinto River and Buffalo Bayou.

Given most Texian volunteers lacked formal training in drill and tactics, Houston wisely used them offensively at San Jacinto. To have permitted a Mexican attack might well have proved disastrous. Instead, he ordered an all-out advance, which took the Mexicans – many of whom had only just arrived after a grueling 24-hour march without food and water – completely by surprise.

San Jacinto is regarded as one of the most decisive battles in military history. The initial fighting lasted about 18 minutes, but the killing of retreating Mexican soldiers lasted much longer. Following the capture of Santa Anna, it was all Houston could do to prevent the Mexican commander from being lynched on the spot. The 959 Texians also had 719 Mexican prisoners to guard and, with their other duties, could have mustered only a small burial party to bury the Mexican dead even if they had been inclined to do so. As it was, 650 Mexican fallen lay unburied on the battlefield.

This leather ammunition pouch and powder horn are believed to have been carried by Private Erastus "Deaf" Smith during his service in the Texian Army. Note the initials "E" and "S" cut into the flap of the pouch. (Phil Collins Texana Collection, courtesy of The Texas General Land Office C-2020-0431)

Aftermath

On receipt of news of the defeat of Santa Anna, interim Mexican President José Justo Corro ordered flags across the country to be lowered to half-staff and draped in mourning. Rejecting the Treaty of Velasco signed by Santa Anna as a prisoner-of-war, which denounced all claims to Texas, he refused to recognize the new Republic. Meanwhile, Filisola was derided for leading the retreat and replaced by Urrea, who within months had gathered 6,000 troops at Matamoros, poised to reconquer Texas. This army was needed to put down continued federalist rebellions in other regions of Mexico, however.

Published in *The Life and Select Literary Remains of Sam Houston of Texas* in 1884, this engraved portrait by George E. Perme, of New York, shows Samuel Houston holding the cane he used to assist in walking as a result of his ankle wound sustained during the battle of San Jacinto. (Author's Collection)

Two further Mexican incursions into Texas took place in 1842. The first, led by General of Brigade Ráfael Vásquez, briefly occupied San Antonio before retiring back across the Rio Grande River. The second, led by the French mercenary General of Brigade Adrián Woll, who was Quartermaster under Santa Anna in 1836, again captured San Antonio but was defeated by Texas Rangers and militia at the battle of Salado Creek on September 17 of that year, following which the invaders retreated into Mexico. Finally, on

June 15, 1843, Houston issued a proclamation declaring an armistice between Texas and Mexico.

Meanwhile, to encourage settlement in the new Republic of Texas, and build a tax base, the Texian government instituted a liberal policy of distributing land to incoming settlers via Headright Certificates, which were divided into categories dependent on whether the settler was a veteran of the Texas Revolution or had arrived in the Republic after the war's end. On December 29, 1845, Texas officially became the 28th state in the Union, although the formal transfer of government did not take place until February 19, 1846. A unique provision in its agreement with the United States permitted Texas to retain title to its public lands, and in 1879 surviving Texian veterans who had served more than three months from October 1, 1835, through January 1, 1837, were guaranteed an additional 1,280 acres in public lands.

After some time in exile in the United States, Santa Anna was permitted to return to Mexico in 1837 and retired to his hacienda in Veracruz. Given command of the Mexican Army again during the Pastry War (1838–39) against the French, he lost a leg in the fighting and had it buried with full military honors. Re-entering politics, he was appointed interim or provisional president six times between 1839 and 1847, and commanded the Mexican Army during the Mexican–American War (1846–48), but renounced the presidency after the fall of Mexico City in September 22, 1847. He was in power for the last time as president with dictatorial powers from 1853 through 1855, but was never again able to lay claim to the title of "Napoleon of the West."

William H. Huddle's 1886 painting depicts General of Division Santa Anna, wearing civilian clothing, surrendering to the wounded Major General Houston the day after the battle of San Jacinto. Other important figures in the scene include the buckskin-clad Texian scout and soldier Private Erastus "Deaf" Smith, seated at bottom right and cupping his ear to hear the proceedings. Tending Houston's wound is Acting Surgeon General Dr. Alexander W. Ewing, while Texian Secretary of War Thomas J. Rusk leans against the oak tree. Having surrendered during the battle, Mexican Colonel Juan Nepomuceno Almonte stands resplendent in his gala uniform next to the reclining Texian general. Captured Mexican battle flags rest against the tree. (Texas State Preservation Board, Capitol Historical Artifact Collection, Austin. Acc # 1989.046)

ORDERS OF BATTLE

The Alamo, March 6, 1836

Texian forces

Total strength: *c.*20 officers and *c.*181 men = *c.*201, plus *c.*18 civilians (servants, women, and children) = *c.*219.

HQ: Lieutenant Colonel William B. Travis, cavalry commander; Colonel James Bowie, infantry commander (sick); Adjutant, Captain John J. Baugh; Chief Ordnance Officer, Major Robert Evans; Assistant Ordnance Officer, Charles Zanco; Assistant Ordnance Officer, Captain Samuel Blair; Chief Engineer, Major Green B. Jameson; Quartermaster, Eliel Melton; Chief Surgeon, Amos Pollard; Captain Albert Martin; Sergeant Major Hiram J. Williamson. Total casualties: *c.*203 KIA, 1 POW and 15 civilian POWs = 219.

Captain Blazeby's Infantry Company: Captain William Blazeby, 1st Lieutenant John Jones, plus *c.*37 men.

James Bowie's Company: Captain William C.M. Baker, Lieutenant Edward McCafferty, plus *c.*17 men.

The Invincibles (Artillery Company): Captain William R. Carey plus *c.*25 men.

Regular Texas Artillery (Chapel Battery): Captain Almeron Dickinson plus *c.*10 men.

Tennessee Mounted Volunteers: Captain William B. Harrison plus *c.*15 men. including David Crockett as nominal commander.

Cavalry Company of Juan Nepomuceno Seguín: *c.*8 men.

Regular Cavalry (Forsyth's Cavalry Company): 1st Lieutenant Cleveland K. Simmons plus *c.*12 men.

Gonzales Ranging Company: Lieutenant George C. Kimball plus *c.*31 men.

Assignment not known, or unassigned: *c.*26 men.

Civilians: *c.*18.

Mexican forces

Total strength in action: 2,117 officers and men. Total casualties: 60 KIA & 251 = 311.

HQ: General of Division Antonio López de Santa Anna; Ramon Martinez Caro, personal secretary; General of Division Vicente Filisola, second-in-command; General of Brigade Juan Arago, chief of staff; Colonel Ricardo Dromundo, purveyor general; Brevet General of Brigade Adrián Woll, quartermaster; Lieutenant Colonel Tomas Requena, chief of artillery; Brevet Lieutenant Colonel Ignacio Labastica, chief of engineers; General of Brigade Manuel Fernandez Castrillon, General of Brigade Martin Perfecto de Cos, General of Brigade Juan Valentin Amador, Colonel Juan Nepomuceno Almonte, Colonel Juan Bringas, and Colonel José Bates, *aides-de-camp.*

Vanguard Brigade: General of Brigade Joaquin Ramirez y Sesma, plus 1,191 officers and men. Total casualties: 26 KIA & 102 WIA.

Matamoros Regular Infantry Battalion: Colonel José Maria Romero and Lieutenant Colonel Manuel Gonzales, plus 275 officers and men. Casualties: 7 KIA & 37 WIA.

Jiménez Regular Infantry Battalion: Lieutenant Colonel Mariano Salas, plus 275 officers and men. Casualties: 9 KIA & 25 WIA.

San Luis Potosí Active Militia Battalion: Colonel Juan Morales, plus 275 officers and men. Casualties: 9 KIA & 37 WIA.

Dolores Regular Cavalry Regiment: Colonel Ventura Marar, plus 285 officers and men. Casualties: 1 KIA & 3 WIA.

Artillery: Lieutenant Colonel Pedro Ampudia, plus 12 officers and 62 men. No casualties.

1st Infantry Brigade: Brevet General of Brigade Antonio Gaona plus 912 men. Total casualties: 34 KIA & 149 WIA.

Aldama Regular Infantry Battalion: Lieutenant Colonel Gregoria Uranuela, plus 340 officers and men. Casualties: 11 KIA & 51 WIA.

Toluca Active Militia Battalion: Colonel Francisco Duque, plus 320 officers and men. Casualties: 20 KIA & 74 WIA.

Sapper Battalion: Lieutenant Colonel Agustín Arnat, plus 19 officers and 185 men. Casualties: 3 KIA & 24 WIA.

Artillery: 63 officers and men with two 12-pounders, two 6-pounders, and two howitzers.

Coleto Creek, March 19–20, 1836

Texian forces

Total strength: *c.*378 officers and men. Total casualties: 7 KIA & *c.*371 POWs including *c.*55 WIA.

HQ: Colonel James W. Fannin, Jr.; Captain John S. Brooks, 1st Lieutenant Joseph M. Chadwick, and Captain Nathaniel R. Brister, adjutants; Sergeant Major Gideon Rose; David I. Holt, quartermaster; Joseph E. Field and Joseph H. Bernard, surgeons. Total casualties: 2 WIA.

Lafayette Battalion: Major Benjamin C. Wallace, plus 291 officers and men. Red Rovers: Captain Jack Shackelford (17 WIA), The Mustangs: Captain Burr H. Duval; San Antonio Greys aka New Orleans Greys: Captain Samuel O. Pettus; Mobile Greys: Captain David N. Burke; Huntsville Volunteers: 1st Lieutenant Benjamin F. Bradford. Casualties: 6 KIA, WIA not known.

Regular Infantry Company: Captain Ira J. Westover, plus 44 officers and men. Casualties: 1 KIA, WIA not known.

Unattached: 32 officers and men, including Texas Regular Artillery under Captain Benjamin H. Holland; and remnants of the Refugio Militia Company of Captain Hugh M. Frazer. Casualties not known.

Mexican forces

Total strength: *c.*1,405 officers and men. Total casualties: *c.*50 KIA & *c.*140 WIA.

HQ: General of Brigade José de Urrea; Lieutenant Colonel Angel Miramón, Lieutenant Colonel Pedro Pablo Ferino, and Captain Mariano Odriosola, *aides-de-camp*; Lieutenant Colonel of Engineers Juan José Holsinger.

1st Infantry Brigade: Lieutenant Colonel Mariano Salas.
Jiménez Regular Infantry Battalion (part): Lieutenant Colonel Mariano Salas, plus 274 officers and men. Casualties not known.
Querétaro Active Militia Battalion: Colonel Cayetana Montoya, plus 375 officers and men. Casualties not known.

2d Infantry Brigade: Colonel Juan Morales.
San Luis Potosí Active Militia Battalion: Colonel Juan Morales. Strength and casualties not known.
Tres Villas Active Militia Battalion: Lieutenant Colonel Agustín Alcerreca, plus 189 officers and men. Casualties not known.
Yucatán Active Militia Battalion: Colonel Nicolas de la Portilla, plus 300 officers and men. Casualties not known.

Elements of the Dolores and Presidial Permanent cavalry units: Colonel Gabriel Núñez, plus 250 officers and men. Casualties not known.
Artillery: Strength and casualties not known.

San Jacinto, April 20–21, 1836

Texian forces

Total strength: 94 officers and 865 men. Total casualties: 7 KIA & 37 WIA.

HQ: Major General Samuel Houston; John A. Wharton, adjutant general; Colonel John Forbes, commissary general; Major William G. Cooke, assistant inspector; Dr. Alexander W. Ewing, acting surgeon general; Major Alexander Horton, Major William H. Patton, and Major James Collinsworth, *aides-de-camp*; Major Lorenzo de Zavala, Major James H. Perry, Captain Robert M. Coleman, and William Massey MD, volunteer aides; Honorable Thomas J. Rusk, Secretary of War; Dr. Junius W. Mottley, aide to Secretary Rusk. Total strength: 14 officers. Casualties: 1 WIA.

1st Regt. Regular Infantry: Lieutenant Colonel Henry W. Millard, plus ten officers and 83 men. No casualties.

1st Regt. Texas Volunteers: Colonel Edward Burleson, plus 24 officers and 362 men. Casualties: 3 KIA & 22 WIA.

2d Regt. Texas Volunteers: Colonel Sidney Sherman, plus 33 officers and 290 men. Total casualties: 2 KIA & 7 WIA.

2d Regt. Texas Volunteers Cavalry Corps: Colonel Mirabeau B. Lamar, plus five officers and 51 men. Total casualties: 1 KIA & 3 WIA.

Artillery: Colonel George W. Hockley, Captain Isaac N. Moreland, 1st Lieutenant William S. Stillwell, and Dr. Nicholas D. Labadie, plus 28 men. Total casualties: 1 WIA.

Mexican forces

Total strength: *c.*1,369 officers and men. Total casualties: *c.*650 KIA & *c.*719 POWs, of whom 208 were WIA.

HQ: General of Division Antonio López de Santa Anna; General of Brigade Manuel Fernandez Castrillon, Colonel Juan Nepomuceno Almonte, and Colonel José Bates, *aides-de-camp*; plus 26 other officers.

Escort Squadron: *c.*60 officers and men of the Dolores and Tampico Regular Cavalry regiments. Casualties not known.

Matamoros Regular Infantry Battalion: Colonel José Maria Romero, plus 240 officers and men. Casualties not known.

Guadalajara Active Militia Battalion: 150 officers and men. Casualties not known.

Grenadier Battalion: *c.*160 officers and men. Grenadier companies of the Guerrero and Aldama Regular Infantry battalions and the Mexico, Toluca, and Guadalajara Active Militia battalions. Casualties not known.

Light Infantry (Cazadores) Battalion: 160 officers and men. Voltigeur companies of the Guerrero and Aldama

Regular Infantry battalions and the Mexico, Toluca, and Guadalajara Active Militia battalions. Casualties not known.

Artillery detachment: Captain Ferdinand Urizza and Lieutenant Ignacio Arrenal, plus 20 men. Casualties: 1 WIA.

Reinforcements: General of Brigade Martin Perfecto de Cos, plus 549 officers and men.

Guerrero Regular Infantry Battalion: Colonel Manuel de Cespedes, plus 160 officers and men. Casualties not known.

Toluca Active Militia Battalion: Colonel Francisco Duque, plus six officers and 83 men. Casualties not known.

Guadalajara Active Militia Battalion: 150 officers and men. Casualties not known.

Aldama Regular Infantry Battalion: 150 officers and men. Casualties not known.

SELECT BIBLIOGRAPHY

Archivo Historico Militar, Government of Mexico (*AHM*).

Baker, B.W.C. (1873). *General Sam Houston, Brief History of Texas from its Earliest Settlement*. New York, NY & Chicago, IL: A.S. Barnes & Co.

Castañeda, Carlos E. (trans. & ed.) (1928). *The Mexican Side of the Texas Revolution*. Dallas, TX: P.L. Turner Co. Castañeda translated "Relations Between Texas, The United States of America and the Mexican Republic" by José María Tornel y Mendivil, which was originally published in Mexico in 1837.

Chartrand, René (1996). "Organization and Uniforms of the Mexican Army, 1810–1838," *Military Collector & Historian* 48.1 (Spring): 2–16.

Collins, Phil (2012). *The Alamo and Beyond: A Collector's Journey*. College Station, TX: Texas A&M University Press.

Daughters of the Republic of Texas Library at the Alamo (DRT), San Antonio, TX. Broadside S-876A, published April 18, 1836.

Davenport Papers, Center for American History, University of Texas at Austin.

Delgado, Pedro (1921). *Mexican Account of the Battle of San Jacinto*. Deepwater, TX: W.C. Day, Superintendent San Jacinto State Park.

Dixon, Sam Houston & Louis Wiltz Kemp (1932). *The Heroes of San Jacinto*. Houston, TX: The Anson Jones Press.

Duval, John C. (1892). *Early Times in Texas*. Austin, TX: Printed and Bound by Eugene von Boeckmann.

Ehrenberg, Herman (1843). *Texas und Seine Revolution*. Leipzig: Vertag von Otto Wigand.

Ehrenberg, Herman (1845). *Fahrten und Schicksale eines Deutschen in Texas*. Leipzig: Vertag von Otto Rigant.

Elliott, Claude (1947). "Alabama and the Texas Revolution," *The Southwestern Historical Quarterly* 50.3 (January): 315–28.

"Memoirs of George Bernard Erath" typescript (1886). Box 2Q507 (SRH1230011729), Briscoe Center for American History, University of Texas at Austin, Austin, TX.

Letter from George Fennell to his brother – November 14, 1836. Special Collections, University of Houston Libraries. University of Houston Digital Library, Houston, TX.

Filisola, Vicente (1848–1849). *Memorias Para la Historia de la Guerra de Tejas.* Vols. 1 & 2. Mexico City, Mexico: Tipographia de R. Rafael, Calle de Cadena num. 13. First Edition.

Filisola, Vicente (1849). *Memorias Para la Historia de la Guerra de Tejas.* Vols. 1 & 2. Mexico: Imprenta de Ignacio Cumplido. Second Edition.

Haeker, Charles M. (1997). *On the Prairie of Palo Alto: Historical Archaeology of the U.S.-Mexican War.* College Station, TX: Texas A&M University Press.

Hanford, Albert (1878). *Albert Hanford's Texas State Register for 1878.* Galveston, TX: A. Hanford

Hansen, Todd (ed.) (2003). *The Alamo Reader: A Study in History.* Mechanicsburg, PA: Stackpole Books.

Hardin, Stephen L. (1994). *Texian Iliad – A Military History of the Texas Revolution.* Austin, TX: University of Texas Press.

Hefter, Joseph (1971). *The Army of the Republic of Texas.* Bellevue, NE: Old Army Press.

Hefter, Joseph (2008) (edited and expanded by Patrick R. Wilson). *The Mexican Soldier 1837–1847: Organization, Dress & Equipment.* Oklahoma, OK: The Virtual Armchair General.

James Monroe Hill Papers 1833–1930, box 2R37 (SRH1230011612). Briscoe Center for American History, University of Texas at Austin, Austin, TX.

Jenkins, John H. (ed.) (1973). *The Papers of the Texas Revolution, 1835–1836.* Ten vols. Austin, TX: Presidial Press.

José Enrique de la Peña narrative (1836). José Enrique De La Peña Collection, Briscoe Center for American History, University of Texas at Austin, Austin, TX.

Alfred Kelso biographical sketch, Kemp Papers. Typescript of letter dated April 30, 1836. The Albert and Ethel Herzstein Library, La Porte, TX.

McArdle, Henry Arthur (1895). The McArdle Notebooks, "The Battle of San Jacinto Notebook," Archives and Information Services Division, Texas State Library and Archives Commission.

Ordenanza Militar Para El Regimen, Disciplina, Subordinacion y Servicio del Ejercito Aumentada Con Las Disosiciones Relativas, Anteriores y Posteriores a la Independencia. (1833). Vol. 1. Mexico City, Mexico: Printed by the Galvan Printing House of Mariano Arevalo, Calle de la Cadena, No. 2.

Prontuario Manual de Infanteria para la instruccion de los cuerpos de la Guardia Nacional (1836). Barcelona, Spain: printed by José Torner.

Reglamento para el Ejercicio y Maniobras de la Caballeria (1825). By Order of the Royal Press, Madrid, Spain.

Reglamento para el Ejercicio y Maniobras de la Infanteria: mandado observar en la Republica Mexicana (1829). Mexico City, Mexico: Galvan Printing House by Mariano Arévalo, No. 2, Calle de Cadena.

Reston, Catherine & Louise Bach (1919). *Tears of the Alamo.* San Marcos, TX: San Marcos Publications.

Smithwick, Noah (1900). *The Evolution of a State or Recollections of Old Texas Days.* Austin, TX: Gammel Book Co.

W.C. Swearingen Letters, Dolph Briscoe Center for American History, The University of Texas at Austin: urn:taro:utexas.cah.02395

Talley, Maj. Michael J. (2002). "Leadership Principles Applied to the Goliad Campaign of 1836." Fort Leavenworth, KS: Thesis presented to the Faculty of the US Army Command and General Staff College.

Thompson, Waddy (1846). *Recollections of Mexico.* New York & London: Wiley and Putnam.

Todish, Tim J. & Terry S. (1998). *Alamo Sourcebook, 1836: A Comprehensive Guide to the Alamo and the Texas Revolution.* Fort Worth, TX: Eakin Press.

Travis, William B. Letter dated February 24, 1836, Texas State Library and Archives, accession # 39.).

Wooton, Dudley G. (ed.) (1898). *A Comprehensive History of Texas, 1685–1897.* Vol. 1. Dallas, TX: William G. Scarff.

Newspapers

Alexandria Gazette, Alexandria, VA (*AG*); *Columbian Centinel*, Boston, MA (*CC*); *Courrier de la Louisiane*, New Orleans, LA (*CDLL*); *Daily Advertiser*, Cleveland, OH (*DA*); *Daily Democratic Statesman*, Austin, TX (*DDS*); *El Dorado Republican*, El Dorado, KS (*EDR*); *Evening Star*, Washington, DC (*ES*); *Huron Reflector*, Norwalk, OH (*HR*); *Lynchburg Virginian*, Lynchburg, VA (*LV*); *Mississippi Free Trader*, Natchez, MS (*MFT*); *National Banner and Nashville Whig*, Nashville, TN (*NB & NW*); *North Carolina Argus*, Wadesborough, NC (*NCA*); *National Daily Intelligencer*, Washington, DC (*NDI*); *New Hampshire Gazette*, Portsmouth, NH (*NHG*); *New Orleans Bee*, New Orleans, LA (*NOB*); *New Orleans Commercial Bulletin*, New Orleans, LA (*NOCB*); *San Antonio Daily Express*, San Antonio, TX (*SADE*); *Texas Sentinel*, Austin, TX (*TS*); *The Herald*, New York City, NY (*TH*).

INDEX

References to illustrations are shown in **bold**.
References to plates are shown in **bold** with
caption pages in brackets, e.g. **54–55**, (56).